HEALTHY LATIN EATING

HEALTHY LATIN EATING

OUR FAVORITE FAMILY RECIPES REMIXED

ANGIE MARTINEZ & ANGELO SOSA

WITH SHIRLEY FAN, MS, RD

PHOTOGRAPHS BY CHRISTINA HOLMES

KYLE BOOKS

To my tía Carmen.
May I touch as many lives as you did.
——————————— *Angelo*

To Livia Franco,
my sweet, sweet grandmother.
You are the heart of our family.
——————————— *Angie*

Published in 2015 by Kyle Books
www.kylebooks.com
general.enquiries@kylebooks.com
Distributed by National Book Network
4501 Forbes Blvd., Suite 200
Lanham, MD 20706
Phone: (800) 462-6420
Fax: (800) 338-4550
customercare@nbnbooks.com

10 9 8 7 6 5 4 3 2 1

ISBN 978-1-909487-18-5

Text © 2015 by Angie Martinez
and Angelo Sosa
Photography © 2015 by Christina Holmes
Book design © 2015 by Kyle Books

Project editor Anja Schmidt
Designer Nicky Collings
Photographer Christina Holmes
Food styling Rebecca Jurkevitch
Prop styling Kalen Kaminski
Copy editor Sarah Scheffel
Production Nic Jones, Gemma John
and Lisa Pinnell

Library of Congress Control Number: 2014948389

Color reproduction by Scanhouse

Printed and bound in China by C&C Offset Printing Co., Ltd.

CONTENTS

INTRODUCTION BY ANGIE MARTINEZ

I'm a born and bred Latina and New Yorker. Music is one of my passions, and I'm blessed to have spent more than twenty years on the radio interviewing top hip-hop and R&B artists from all over the world.

In addition to music, I'm also passionate about food. And as a third-generation Latina with roots in Cuba, the Dominican Republic, and Puerto Rico, I love Latin food. If I could eat rice and beans every day, I'd be the happiest girl in the world.

For me, eating Latin food always brings back memories of my childhood and family. As a kid, every Saturday morning I'd take the two-hour subway ride from Brooklyn to Dyckman Street in Manhattan, a few blocks from my Cuban-Dominican grandmother's apartment. By the time I got there, the air in her kitchen was already filled with the smell of *sofrito* and chopped vegetables. All morning long, she'd buzz around prepping her weekly feast of *chulettas* (fried pork chops), empanadas, and fried plantains for all of us. And let me tell you, her food was amazing!

Grandma's kitchen was always the center of family activity. While she cooked, I spent hours by the window, taking in the sights, sounds, and scents of Washington Heights. If we weren't eating, we were getting ready for the next meal. And when we ate, we'd do it in shifts because there were so many of us. Grandma's place was always a crazy scene, but her food brought us together.

But as much as I love Latin food, I know I can't have it every day. So much of the food is deep-fried and packed with meat and empty carbs. And many of the traditional dishes are high in calories, fat, and sodium.

As a single mom trying to balance my hectic schedule with a healthy lifestyle, it pains me to know the food of my childhood is wreaking havoc on my body. And I think a lot of other Latinos feel the same way. Many of us have similar memories of our mothers and grandmothers making these delicious foods, but feel like we can't eat them anymore. I wanted to find a way to enjoy the foods I grew up with, without the side order of guilt. That's why my talented chef friend, Angelo, and I are here to give Latin food a remix.

Our manager set up the meeting between Angelo and me. Of course I looked him up online and he seemed so intimidating in his chef's gear, arms crossed—I'm not going to lie, I was a little afraid. But then we met in the elevator on the ride up to his office and he could not have been more sweet and charming. I knew he was it, and not only has he taught me so much about cooking, but we've become great friends. And after spending so much time with Angelo at his restaurant, Añejo, we've decided to open a second one together! So he's not getting rid of me anytime soon.

BROWN RICE, PLEASE

It might sound strange, but the idea for cooking healthier Latin food came to me as I was eating at a typical American fast-casual restaurant—not exactly a mecca of Latin cuisine. As I scanned the menu for a salad or a grilled piece of anything, I stumbled upon a side of "brown rice and black beans." Now, this was the kind of restaurant that serves chicken fingers and spinach dip, so I wasn't exactly expecting my grandmother's *arroz con frijoles*. But I was intrigued. When the dish came to the table, there wasn't anything particularly Latin about it…but it was good!

This side dish got me thinking about how simple changes can make a big difference. I had read about how brown rice has more nutrients and fiber than white, so why not try similar tweaks in traditional dishes like *arroz con gandules* or *arroz con pollo*? Hey, maybe I was on to something!

So, my adventure in healthier cooking began. I started tweaking all of my favorite Latin dishes. And when I started telling other people about it, I realized that I wasn't the only one trying to cook healthy Latin food! In fact, a lot of my friends were also experimenting with their family recipes and making small changes with big health benefits.

WHAT IS LATIN AMERICAN CUISINE?

Latin America is a region comprised of Mexico, the Caribbean, and Central and South Americas. Because the area is so expansive, the food is highly diverse and inclusive of many different cuisines, such as Peruvian, Mexican, and Cuban.

FEEDING THE NEXT GENERATION

As much as I love food and music, my biggest passion is my eleven-year-old son, Niko. He is the sweetest kid, and loves to help me cook. As a working mom, it's tough to find the time, but I love teaching him the tricks I've learned. And the more Niko helps me cook, the more willing he is to try new foods. Working together in the kitchen has made it easier for both of us to live a healthier lifestyle.

It's a great feeling to know we're eating healthier as a family, but there's still a lot of work to do in the greater Latino community. At Niko's little league games in the Bronx, it feels like the only foods available are fried and fatty. Now I love empanadas or *chicharon* (fried chicken chunks) as much as the next girl, but when you look around and see that so many kids are twenty to thirty pounds overweight, the connection is hard to ignore. The attitude among Latino parents is usually like, "This is the food we eat and the way we like it. There aren't any other options." But to me, there's clearly something wrong. How can we be role models to our children if we don't eat well ourselves? And how do we change these habits before it's too late?

Many of us in the Latino community have personally been affected by this problem. I was at my friend Fat Joe's house and we talked about all these big guys in our industry that we've lost to obesity. Big Pun was one who stood out. He was such a talented rapper, and had a whole career ahead of him. But sadly, he passed way from a heart attack when he was just twenty-eight. I think it was that conversation that made me realize something needed to be done to help the community and our children.

Starting my own blog, HealthyLatinEating.com, was the first step in helping out. On the site, I curate healthy recipes and articles from bloggers around the country. Receiving people's enthusiastic responses from all over made me realize just how much demand there is for healthier Latin food.

CHANGING LIFESTYLES, NOT DIETS

I didn't want to write a diet book filled with calorie counts and grams of fat. I've spent most of my life dieting, from Jenny Craig to Weight Watchers to Atkins to Scarsdale, and none of them have worked for me—not for long, anyway! Now that I'm older (and hopefully wiser), I don't let my weight stress me out as much. Instead of jumping on the latest diet fad, I focus my efforts on making positive lifestyle changes that include eating real and good food!

This book is meant to be a guide for people who are looking for healthy, amazingly delicious Latin recipes, and helpful tips for lightening up their own favorite dishes. As I mentioned earlier, I've partnered with Angelo Sosa, a supremely talented chef (who also makes a mean margarita!), to help transform the traditional foods that we ate at our family tables into healthy dishes that are not only delicious, but have the same spice, flavor, and love as the originals.

Throughout the chapters, we've created a collection of recipes that celebrates both Latin cooking and healthy eating. Beyond family treasures like Ensalada de Carmen (page 62), Crispy Tostones (page 32), and Niko's Tropical Smoothie (page 171), we've also included innovative dishes like Shrimp and Papaya Ceviche (page 35) and Silken Soy and Almond Milk Flan (page 147). Every recipe draws from traditional Latin ingredients, like nutty coriander seed, aromatic cilantro, and earthy cumin, while incorporating a new healthy twist, such as replacing rice with quinoa. And by using these health-conscious substitutions of fresh ingredients, alternative cooking methods, and little tweaks to the sugar, fat, and sodium content, we've created lighter fare that still captures the fun and passion of Latin cooking.

As a bonus, my friends DJ Enuff, John Leguizamo, Jorge Posada, Robinson Cano, Rosie Perez, Fat Joe, Henry Santos, and Adrienne Bailon have pitched in and shared the kinds of foods they enjoy at home. And I'm honored that even the estate of Celia Cruz has given me a recipe that the legendary singer used to make. Let me tell you, all of these recipes are super tasty!

It's our hope that with this book, we can help empower people to make better food choices and to open up conversation at the family table about what small changes can be made together. It's time to realize that our families' recipes don't need to be fried in lard or served in huge portions just because that's the way it's always been. It's time we remix our foods and teach the new generation how to eat well, while enjoying ourselves too! So enough of my talking, let's get to the kitchen, or as we say in Spanish, *vamos a la cocina*!

THE HEALTH OF LATINOS

Food is important to Latino culture, but it's also working against us. According to the U.S. Census Bureau, Latinos are one of the fastest growing minority groups in the United States. But recent statistics also show that Latinos are 1.2 times more likely to be obese and 1.7 times more likely to be diagnosed with diabetes than non-Latinos (U.S. Department of Health and Human Services Office of Minority Health).

ANGELO'S HEALTHY KITCHEN
COCINA SALUDABLE

I grew up in a small New England town in a large Dominican-Italian family. My Dominican father did all the cooking at home, and I was his little sous chef. A military man, he was very strict and meticulous. If I washed the rice, it had to be clean. Besides teaching me discipline in the kitchen, my father also exposed me to a host of Latin flavors that were unusual and exciting, specifically a sweet red bean pudding for Easter and a drink called *beruga*, made from fermented sour milk.

My father taught me how to be a skilled technician in the kitchen, but it was my *tía* Carmen who instilled in me the passion and love for food. As a kid, I'd go to her house in Queens, sit on a barstool in the kitchen, and watch her cook for hours with my mouth wide open. Her *tostones*, rice and beans, and *bacalao* with green olives taught me that cooking can be a powerful vehicle for showing love to others. Even after working with so many top chefs around the world, I still look to her as an inspiration for how I want to cook.

I take great pride in being Latino. Looking back, I have such an appreciation for all those hours spent in my family's Latin kitchens, my childhood visits to the Dominican Republic, and the exposure I gained to many unique flavors and ingredients. These experiences developed my palate, and gave me a curiosity about the world. And today, I draw upon those experiences in my role as chef-owner of Añejo, a modern Mexican tequileria, in New York City.

When I think about Latin cuisine, I imagine flavorful food, made from the heart that touches the soul. It's vibrant, dynamic, and approachable. But as Angie mentioned, it also has a reputation for being unhealthy. So, when she came to me with the idea of promoting healthy Latin food, I couldn't say no. As a chef and a father, I love the idea of supporting the well-being of future generations through cooking.

A TRINITY OF FLAVORS

In order to develop healthier renditions of traditional recipes, I went back to a core principle of my cooking philosophy: the trinity of flavors. The idea is that you

highlight three different flavor profiles (or components) in a dish that work in harmony with each other to make it taste outstanding. As an example, in Sweet & Sour Mango Guava Salad (page 65), the mangoes have a sweet flavor, while the fish sauce adds a salty element. But it's the sour lime and yuzu juices that complete the trinity and make this salad sing. In the end, you have sweet, salty, and sour flavors that complement each other and make an intensely complex dish. You can do this with any variety of flavors; just choose a complementary trio to elevate a dish and knock it right out of the park.

Too often in Latin cooking, the focus on heavy, stick-to-your-ribs ingredients results in one-dimensional dishes with muddled flavors. My goal for this book was to isolate the strong tastes in each dish, amplify them, and add more harmonious flavors to create a trinity. Take for example, *tostones*—fried plantains seasoned with salt. Now, everybody loves *tostones*, but they are a one-note item. So, why not take crushed garlic and rub that on the chips? And while the plantains are hot, how about throwing some crushed bay leaves into the mix? Besides salt, you've now flavored the dish with garlic and bay leaf, giving it a salty, astringent, and floral profile (see Crispy Tostones, page 32).

FLAVOR, FLAVOR, FLAVOR!

A key reason why people overeat is because they're not satisfied. If we can extract more flavor out of ingredients and create pleasing combinations like my flavor trinity, then we will be more satisfied with a little less.

The first step is to buy fresh ingredients. This doesn't mean that you need to spend outrageous amounts of money at specialty foods stores. Just consider the food that you are buying. How far away from where it was grown is it? I grew up next to a cornfield, and I can tell you that the difference between canned corn and a fresh cob is like night and day. Store-bought Latin foods are often processed for longer shelf lives, leaving much to be desired in terms of flavor, so it's important to start thinking outside the grocery aisles. If your grocery store has great produce, great! But if not, check out a farmers' market or even the local corner store for fresh and flavorful vegetables and fruit without any additives.

The second step is to use herbs and spices for flavor instead of fat. Latin food already uses a heavy dose of these flavorings, so why not take advantage of that? One way to do this is to toast spices, which helps them release their flavor-rich oils. But use fresh herbs whenever possible—compared to dried herbs, they give off a brighter, livelier flavor.

LIGHTEN UP WITH THESE COOKING TECHNIQUES

Steaming: Cooking foods like vegetables with steam helps retain their texture, color, taste, and nutrients. An easy way to steam food is to put it on a rack or in a steamer basket over boiling water and cover it. Or wrap food in parchment paper or banana leaves and then place it in an oven or over a grill. The food will cook from the steam created by its own juices.

Sautéing: This dry heat cooking method requires the least amount of oil to be added to the pan. Simply add a small amount of olive oil to a hot pan and then add your ingredients. Quick cooking ensures that the food retains some texture, color, and nutrients.

Baking: Oven-baking is a great alternative to frying. You can get similar crunchy results from baking in the oven as you would by frying—but without all the fat.

Grilling: Like sautéing, grilling uses a minimal amount of fat. Food is cooked directly on a hot grill that's been lightly swiped with a paper towel sprinkled with vegetable oil, leaving it with a smoky, charred flavor.

Broiling: This oven technique is similar to grilling except that the heat source comes from above, rather than underneath. Broiling gives food a charred and crispy texture. It's also very accessible—just crank up the oven.

EASY IDEAS FOR HEALTHY SUBSTITUTIONS

Want white rice? Try more nutrient-rich grains like barley, brown rice, quinoa (in all different colors), and whole-wheat couscous.

Say good-bye to lard with healthier oils like olive, canola or vegetable, and grapeseed, which has a higher smoke point and won't impart an olive oil taste.

Swap white flour tortillas for whole grain, whole-wheat, or corn tortillas; all are available at most supermarkets. Or reduce the calories by using lettuce wraps instead.

Cut down on saturated fat by choosing leaner meats like skinless chicken breast, turkey, or pork tenderloin. Meatless options include tofu, beans, and tempeh. Add flavor with herbs and spices instead of fat.

Use plain Greek yogurt for a protein-rich topping instead of sour cream.

Replace mayonnaise with mashed avocado.

GO-TO INGREDIENTS

To make great Latin food, I recommend keeping the following ingredients on hand. Although many can be found in supermarkets in the produce and international food sections, you can also source these ingredients online at sites like kalustyans.com, amazon.com, and melissas.com.

PANTRY/DESPENSA

Agave nectar: Native to Mexico, agave is one and a half times sweeter than sugar. It has a thin, viscous texture and imparts a light caramel flavor to dishes and drinks. Most importantly, I like it because it's indigenous to Latin American cuisine. Use it sparingly, as it's still a source of calories.

Guava paste: This thick, sweet, deep red paste is made from guava, a tropical fruit found throughout Latin America and the Caribbean. Buy the paste in tins or round disks for use in vinaigrettes, glazes, or desserts. To make your own, see page 64.

Cumin: Found in seed or powder form, cumin has a musty flavor that is great in recipes for guacamole, stews, dressings, and more. I like to toast it to boost its flavor and aroma.

Capers and olives: You'll need a small amount of these two ingredients to give dishes a punch of briny flavor. Go for the brined varieties and save the liquid for vinaigrettes.

Beans: Dried or canned beans are an inexpensive source of protein and fiber. I stock both kinds in my kitchen. Dried are marvelous because they're inexpensive and versatile. Canned works well if you don't have a lot of time. Make sure to rinse canned beans before using to remove excess sodium. Keep them on hand for dips, soups, and stews.

REFRIGERATOR/REFRIGERADOR

Thyme: I use this member of the mint family fresh or dried to build a foundation of flavor in dishes.

Cilantro: An essential part of Latin cuisine, cilantro has a fresh, citrusy taste that brightens up any dish, whether cooked or presented as a garnish.

Bay leaf: I prefer fresh, but use what you can find. It has a very floral flavor that rounds out dishes and makes them magical. Use it for everything, from salads to stews, or you can infuse oils and vinegars with it.

COUNTER/ENCIMERA

Garlic: Buy firm bulbs and store them in a cool, dry place. Avoid chopped garlic in jars because it picks up a processed flavor.

Avocados: Choose firm avocados with no blemishes on the skin. If underripe, place next to ripe bananas or apples. Apples and bananas release ethylene, a gas that can speed up the ripening of an avocado.

Pineapple: Look for firm, fresh-looking, fragrant fruit with green leaves. Use in sweet and savory dishes, and save the rinds for their tenderizing effect in meat braises.

Plantains: These starchy tropical fruits resemble large bananas, but must be cooked before eating. To buy, gently squeeze the fruit to check for ripeness; green ones should be firm; yellow ones should yield to pressure; black ones should feel soft. Avoid cracked or moldy plantains.

Mango: Mangoes are incredibly versatile and make great additions to salsas, drinks, and desserts. Select blemish-free mangoes and allow them to ripen at room temperature. Ripe ones will be fragrant and give a little when squeezed. After they are ripe, store them in the refrigerator.

Lime: Fresh lime juice is essential for brightening up dishes. Don't bother with the bottled stuff. The flavors are muted and lack the freshness and vibrancy we want.

Small bites and appetizers set the tone for the meal to come, and are a great opportunity to experiment with different tastes in one sitting. We've included a variety of small dishes that are full of color and packed with flavor. Serve them as an intro to a meal, or pair them with a nice green salad for a light lunch or dinner. Everything in this chapter can be easily made at home, so don't be afraid to try multiple recipes at a time. You can even try serving a bunch at once for a tapas-like spread, which is what we love to do!

SMALL PLATES

Platos Pequeños

GRILLED CORN ON THE COB

— Angelo

Growing up in a small farming town in Connecticut, I have great memories of picking fresh corn with my father. I was always at his side in the kitchen, so go figure that it was my job to shuck the corn! All the labor was worth it—the sweet flavor and crisp texture of the corn was refreshing in the summer heat. I've lightened up this family heirloom recipe by slathering the corn with extra-virgin olive oil instead of butter and spicing it up with smoky chipotle salt.

SERVES: 4
TIME: 30 MINUTES

4 ears fresh corn, shucked
2 tablespoons extra-virgin
   olive oil
1 tablespoon chipotle chile
   powder
2 tablespoons kosher salt
1 lime, cut into quarters

Preheat an outdoor grill or grill pan to medium-high.

Put the corn in a large pot of water over medium-high heat. Bring to a boil, then reduce the heat to a simmer. Cook until the corn is tender, about 10 minutes, then drain.

Brush the olive oil over the corn and grill, turning occasionally, until nicely charred on all sides, 5 to 10 minutes total. While the corn grills, combine the chipotle powder and salt in a small bowl.

Remove the corn from the grill and season with the chipotle salt. Serve with lime wedges.

CORN WITH SALSA VERDE

— Angelo

I might be a little biased toward grilled corn on the cob because I grew up next to a cornfield, but there's something magical about its smoky aroma. At home, we'd slather it with butter and top it with this salsa verde, which provides a spicy kick and brightens up the corn with its herbaceous notes. Here we skip the butter for a healthier version.

SERVES: 4
TIME: 25 MINUTES

4 ears fresh corn, shucked
2 tablespoons extra-virgin
   olive oil
1 teaspoon kosher salt
2 fresh jalapeños, minced
2 tablespoons capers,
   rinsed and chopped
2 tablespoons chopped
   fresh cilantro
¼ cup thinly sliced scallions
3 tablespoons green
   Tabasco sauce

Preheat an outdoor grill or grill pan to medium-high.

Bring a large pot of water to a boil over medium-high heat. Gently add the corn, olive oil, and salt, return to a boil, then reduce the heat to a simmer. Cook until the corn is tender, about 10 minutes.

Meanwhile, stir together the rest of the ingredients in a small bowl.

Drain, then grill the corn, turning occasionally, until nicely charred on all sides, 5 to 10 minutes. To serve, spoon the salsa verde over the corn.

GARLIC & GOLDEN RAISIN GAZPACHO

Angelo

We tend to think of gazpacho as a chilled red soup, made from tomatoes, onions, peppers, and cucumbers, but in certain regions of Spain, they serve a blond one. Made from garlic, almonds, and golden raisins, this paler cousin is equally delectable. In this version, I use whole-wheat baguette to add more vitamins, minerals, and fiber.

SERVES: 4
TIME: 20 MINUTES

3 to 4 (1-inch-thick) slices
    stale whole-wheat baguette
8 cloves garlic, peeled
½ cup blanched almonds
5 tablespoons olive oil, plus
    more for drizzling
3 tablespoons sherry vinegar,
    plus more to taste
3 tablespoons golden raisins
kosher salt

Trim the crust from the bread. Soak in a deep plate filled with 1 to 2 cups cold water. Squeeze the liquid from the bread, reserving the water. Set aside.

Place the garlic and almonds in the bowl of a food processor. Pulse until smooth. Tear the bread into quarters and add to the garlic mixture. Process until smooth, scraping down the sides if necessary. While blending, slowly add the olive oil, vinegar, and finally the raisins. Add the reserved soaking water if the soup seems dry. Season with up to 1 tablespoon additional vinegar and salt to taste.

Chill for 1 hour. Garnish with a drizzle of olive oil and serve.

WATERMELON GAZPACHO

Angelo

SERVES: 4 TO 6
TIME: 40 MINUTES

2 cups roughly chopped
    watermelon
2 cups roughly chopped ripe
    tomato
¼ cup roughly chopped
    cucumber
¼ cup roughly chopped
    red onion
¼ cup roughly chopped green
    bell pepper
1 Thai (or bird's eye) chile
    pepper
¼ cup red wine vinegar
1 teaspoon kosher salt,
    plus more to taste
¼ cup sugar
2 basil leaves, torn

A traditional gazpacho is made with bread, which adds unnecessary carbs to the dish. In this sweet, sour, and herbaceous version, we've added watermelon, which keeps you hydrated in the summer heat and packs vitamins like A and C into the dish. All of these fresh vegetables along with the sweet watermelon make this a garden lover's delight.

Chill the blender container for at least 30 minutes.

Combine the watermelon, tomato, cucumber, onion, bell pepper, chile, vinegar, salt and sugar in the blender and blend to a coarse texture. Taste for seasoning, adding more salt if necessary. Chill for at least 1 hour.

To serve, pour into chilled bowls and garnish with the basil.

"It was genius of Angelo to put watermelon in this dish. Even though gazpacho is already pretty light, the addition of watermelon makes it fresher and gives it sweetness I absolutely love."

——————————————— *Angie*

CUBAN MEDIANOCHE EMPANADAS

Angie

Inspired by my Cuban-Dominican grandmother, Livia, I've been making empanadas for years. She makes hers with a ground beef mixture, known as *picadillo*, and then fries the little babies up in oil. To lighten up her recipe, remix these by filling them with citrus-braised pork (a nod to the Cubano sandwich) and bake them. You still get a flaky, delicious crust, but you don't get all the grease and heaviness that comes with frying.

MAKES: 14 EMPANADAS
TIME: ABOUT 3 HOURS 30 MINUTES, PLUS CHILLING AND COOLING

BASIC EMPANADA DOUGH
3 cups all-purpose flour, plus more for dusting
2 egg yolks
¼ cup water
6 tablespoons olive oil

CITRUS-BRAISED PORK FILLING
1 (2½-pound) bone-in pork shoulder, trimmed of most visible fat

To make the empanada dough, in a medium bowl, mix all the ingredients together until it forms a firm ball. Transfer the dough onto a floured surface and knead until smooth. Form the dough into a ball and tightly wrap in plastic wrap. Refrigerate for at least 20 minutes, or up to 2 days. When wrapped well, this dough can also be frozen for up to 3 months.

When you're ready to make the pork filling, preheat the oven to 350°F.

Rub the pork with the cumin, coriander, and 1½ tablespoons each of salt and pepper. Heat the oil in a large heavy-bottomed pot or Dutch oven over medium-high heat. When the oil is shimmering, brown the pork on all the sides, about 3 minutes per side. Add the chicken stock, vinegar, coarsely chopped onion, garlic, orange and lime juices, bay leaves, thyme, and oregano. Cover the pot and place in the oven to braise for 1 to 2 hours, until the meat easily comes off the bone.

1½ tablespoons ground cumin

1½ tablespoons ground coriander

kosher salt and freshly ground black pepper

2 tablespoons canola or vegetable oil

1½ cups chicken stock

1 tablespoon sherry vinegar

1 large onion, coarsely chopped, plus ¼ cup finely chopped onion

½ head garlic, peeled and chopped

½ cup orange juice

¼ cup fresh lime juice (from about 2 limes)

1½ fresh or dried bay leaves

4 sprigs fresh thyme

1½ sprigs fresh oregano

½ tablespoon Dijon mustard

2 tablespoons finely chopped cilantro

2 tablespoons olive oil

nonstick cooking spray

1 egg, lightly beaten, for brushing

Remove the pork from the oven and let cool. Shred the cooled pork into small pieces and place in a bowl. Strain the cooking liquid through a fine-mesh sieve and transfer to a medium saucepan. Over medium-high heat, cook the liquid until it's reduced down to one third. Whisk in the mustard and season with salt and pepper. Pour over the shredded pork and let rest for at least 2 hours before folding in the finely chopped onion, cilantro, and olive oil.

When you're ready to assemble and bake the empanadas, preheat the oven to 350°F. Spray 2 sheet trays with nonstick cooking spray. Remove the bay leaves and thyme and rosemary sprigs from the pork. Fill a small bowl with water and place it nearby. Roll out the dough to about ¼-inch thickness. Using a 3½-inch-diameter round biscuit cutter, cut out 14 circles. Place about 1 tablespoon of the pork filling near the center of a round of dough. Dip your finger in the bowl of water and dab around the edges of the dough. Fold the dough in half over the filling, pressing the edges together. Crimp the edges and poke the tops a few times with the tines of a fork. Brush the tops with the egg wash and bake until golden brown, 18 to 20 minutes.

YUCCA EMPANADA
WITH CHIPOTLE SALT

Angelo

Empanadas are delicious filled pastries that you can eat on the run or enjoy as a side or snack. In this dish, I wanted to show the diversity of empanada fillings you can prepare by using yucca, a starchy root vegetable with an earthy flavor. This is a departure from the typical empanada, which contains meat. If you like, make a full recipe of empanada dough and use half for this recipe and the other half for the Salted Cod Empanadas opposite.

MAKES: 7 EMPANADAS
TIME: 1 HOUR 30 MINUTES,
PLUS CHILLING AND COOLING

½ recipe Basic Empanada
   Dough (page 20)
1 tablespoons chipotle chile
   powder
2 teaspoons kosher salt
2 cups peeled and chopped
   yucca (see page 47)
1 teaspoon olive oil
3 tablespoons chopped onion
2 tablespoons distilled white
   vinegar
½ teaspoon chopped fresh
   thyme
nonstick cooking spray
2 egg yolks, beaten

Prepare the empanada dough through chilling, as on page 20. In a small bowl, combine the chipotle powder and salt. Set aside.

In a medium saucepan over medium-high heat, combine the yucca with 4 cups water. Bring to a boil, then lower the heat and simmer until the yucca is tender, 20 to 30 minutes. Strain.

In a medium sauté pan, heat the olive oil over medium heat. When hot, add the onion and cook until softened, about 5 minutes. Add the yucca and vinegar and cook until the flavors meld, 5 to 8 minutes. Season with 1 teaspoon of the chipotle salt, stir in the thyme and remove from the heat. Let cool.

Preheat the oven to 350°F. Spray a sheet tray with nonstick cooking spray. Place the bowl of beaten egg yolks and a brush nearby.

Lightly flour a work surface and roll out the dough into a ¼-inch-thick rectangle. Using a 6-inch-diameter biscuit cutter, cut out 7 rounds of dough. Place 1 tablespoon of the filling in the center of each round. Brush the edges of the circles with egg yolk and fold the dough in half to create half moons. Fold the edges over to seal. Brush the tops with the egg yolk.

Arrange the empanadas on the prepared sheet tray and chill for 20 minutes. Bake until golden brown on top, about 20 minutes.

SALTED COD EMPANADA

Angelo

You can fill empanadas with just about anything, from leftovers to sweet or salty mixtures. In this recipe, I opt for salt cod, a staple in Latin American cooking and an ingredient that still exemplifies this ancient technique for preserving food. It might look (and smell) a bit daunting, but it's a delicious ingredient that should not be regarded with fear.

MAKES: 7 EMPANADAS
TIME: 50 MINUTES, PLUS CHILLING AND COOLING

½ recipe Basic Empanada Dough (page 20)
3 tablespoons olive oil
¼ cup finely diced onion
¼ cup finely diced red bell pepper
¼ cup finely diced green bell pepper
½ cup chopped fresh tomato
1 teaspoon paprika
½ teaspoon chipotle chile powder
2 teaspoons chopped fresh thyme leaves
1 fresh or dried bay leaf
1 tablespoon chopped fresh cilantro
½ pound salt cod, soaked in water for 2 to 4 hours and drained
1 tablespoon red wine vinegar
nonstick cooking spray
2 egg yolks, beaten

Prepare the empanada dough through chilling, as on page 20.

In a large pan over medium heat, add the olive oil. When hot, add the onion, bell peppers, and tomato and cook until softened and aromatic, 3 to 5 minutes. Add the paprika, chipotle powder, thyme, bay leaf, cilantro, and salt cod and cook for another 5 minutes. Add the vinegar and cook for 2 minutes more, tossing all the ingredients together. Remove from the heat and let cool to room temperature, about 30 minutes.

When ready to make the empanadas, preheat the oven to 350°F. Spray a sheet tray with nonstick cooking spray. Remove the bay leaf from the filling.

Lightly flour a work surface and roll out the dough into a ¼-inch-thick rectangle. Using a 6-inch-diameter biscuit cutter, cut out 7 dough rounds. Place 1 tablespoon of the filling in the center of each round. Brush the edges with the beaten egg yolk and fold the dough in half to create half moons. Fold the edges over and pinch to seal. Brush the tops with egg yolk.

Place the empanadas on the prepared sheet tray and chill for 20 minutes. Bake in the oven until golden brown on top, about 20 minutes.

"Since I love salted cod and empanadas, putting them together in this dish is like the best of both worlds. They're totally delicious. We always fried empanadas in my family growing up, but these are baked and guilt-free."

— Angie

DOMINICAN QUIPES

Angelo

Although it's a small nation, historically the Dominican Republic has been populated by people from all over the world. *Quipes* are deep-fried snacks adapted from Middle Eastern immigrants—meat and bulgur croquettes that resemble the Syrian and Lebanese kibbeh. I love the Dominican interpretation of the dish, but to make it lighter, I use lean ground turkey and bake it instead of frying. It's just as delicious!

SERVES: 7 (2 CROQUETTES EACH)
TIME: 50 MINUTES

1 tablespoon vegetable oil, plus more for greasing
1 cup bulgur wheat
1 small red onion
1 medium green bell pepper
1¼ pounds lean ground turkey
kosher salt and freshly ground black pepper
pinch of chopped fresh oregano
1 tablespoon tomato paste
2 leaves fresh basil, finely chopped
¼ cup raisins

Preheat the oven to 350°F. Grease two sheet pans with vegetable oil.

Place the bulgur in a small pot, cover with water, and bring to a boil. Cook until tender, 10 to 15 minutes, adding more water to cover if necessary, then rinse under cold water. Drain the wheat in a fine-mesh sieve, squeezing any water out. Set aside.

Chop the onion into ¼-inch dice. Seed the bell pepper, and then chop into small pieces about the same size as the onion. In a medium bowl, mix the onion and bell pepper with the ground turkey. Season with 1 teaspoon salt and a pinch each of black pepper and oregano. Mix well.

Heat 1 tablespoon oil in a shallow pan over medium heat. Add one-third of the meat mixture, stirring to break it up. Add 2 tablespoons water and the tomato paste and reduce the heat to low. Simmer until the meat is cooked through, 5 to 10 minutes, adding more water if the mixture looks too dry. Fold in the basil and raisins, and season with salt. Cool to room temperature.

In a large bowl, mix the uncooked meat mixture with the bulgur. Put 2 to 3 tablespoons of the bulgur mixture in the palm of a wet hand. Flatten it and then put 1 tablespoon of the cooked meat mixture in the center. Roll the bulgur mixture over the meat to encase it and form a football-shaped croquette. Repeat with the remaining bulgur and meat mixtures to form about 14 croquettes.

Place the balls on the prepared sheet pans and bake for 15 to 20 minutes. Serve warm.

CORN TAMALES
STEAMED IN BANANA LEAVES

Angelo

Tamales are traditionally made with lard, so to lighten them up, I use olive oil. This version still retains the essence of the traditional tamale, but eliminates all the heart-stopping saturated fat that comes with rendered pork fat. With all the incredible flavor from the cheese and chiles, you won't miss the lard at all. To liven them up, I also use banana leaves for their subtle flavor (you can find them in Latin markets) and corn kernels for their textural impact.

SERVES: 4 TO 6
TIME: 1 HOUR 50 MINUTES

2 cups masa harina (see below opposite)
2 cups hot water
2 tablespoons olive oil
2 tablespoons chopped Oaxaca cheese (see below opposite)
1 cup fresh or frozen corn kernels
1 teaspoon chopped chipotle in adobo
2 tablespoons minced jalapeño
1 teaspoon kosher salt
4 to 6 banana leaves, rinsed and trimmed into 8 × 10-inch rectangles
2 tablespoons grated Cotija cheese (see below opposite)

Place the masa harina and hot water in a medium bowl and beat until completely blended. Stir in the olive oil. Set aside for 30 minutes to cool.

In a small bowl, stir together the Oaxaca cheese, corn, chipotle, jalapeño, and salt.

When you're ready to assemble the tamales, lay the banana leaves out on a countertop and divide the masa mixture equally among the leaves. Place the corn and cheese mixture in the middle of the masa, dividing it equally among the tamales. Bring the two long sides of a leaf and fold one over the other so that the masa and corn mixtures are encased. Fold the two remaining sides under the tamale. As long as the leaf is securely folded, you do not need to tie with string. Repeat with the remaining leaves.

Place the bundles tucked-side down in a steamer basket set over a pot of simmering water. Steam for 1 hour. Check the water periodically and refill if necessary. The tamales are done when the leaves can be easily peeled away.

Let the tamales sit for 10 minutes before serving. To serve, split open the top of the bundles to reveal the filling and sprinkle with Cotija cheese.

CALABAZA TAMALES

Angelo

Calabaza is a colorful squash popular throughout Latin America. It's frequently used in soups, stews, sauces, and breads, and is a source of beta-carotene, potassium, and vitamin C. Because of its firm but moist texture, I thought it would make an excellent filling for this meatless tamale. Buy calabaza whole or chopped up in Latin markets.

SERVES: 4
TIME: 1 HOUR 30 MINUTES, PLUS SOAKING AND COOLING

9 dried corn husks
2 cups masa harina (see below)
2 cup hot water
2 tablespoons olive oil
1 cup finely chopped calabaza or pumpkin
1 teaspoon kosher salt
¼ cup chopped Oaxaca cheese (see below)
2 teaspoons finely chopped chipotle in adobe
¼ cup minced jalapeño

In a medium bowl, cover the corn husks with hot water. Let soak for at least 30 minutes to soften the husks.

Place the masa harina and hot water in another medium bowl and beat until completely blended. Stir in the olive oil. Set aside for 30 minutes to cool.

Add the pumpkin, salt, cheese, chipotle, and jalapeño to the masa harina.

When you're ready to assemble the tamales, tear one of the corn husks into 8 strips. Equally divide the pumpkin mixture among the remaining corn husks, leaving a 1-inch border at the tapered end of each husk and around the sides. Wrap each tamale by bringing in the two long sides and rolling the bundle up. Tie up the bundle with a strip of corn husk.

Place the tamales in a steamer basket set over a pot of simmering water. Steam for 1 hour. Check the water periodically and refill if necessary. The tamales are done when the husk can be easily peeled away. Let the tamales sit for 10 minutes before serving.

WHAT IS OAXACA CHEESE?

Mild and mellow, Oaxaca cheese is the Mexican equivalent of mozzarella. It's a cow's milk cheese made by kneading and stretching the curds to form a rope. Because it melts well, it's used to make round sandwiches called *cemitas* and Mexican fondue, also known as *queso fundito*. You can source it in many Latin markets, but feel free to use mozzarella cheese as a substitute.

WHAT IS COTIJA CHEESE?

An aged cow's milk cheese named after the town of Cotija in Mexico, Cotija is white and has a dry and crumbly texture. Salty and strongly flavored, Cotija does not melt and is often served crumbled on top of dishes. It's nicknamed the "Parmesan of Mexico."

WHAT IS MASA HARINA?

Translated to "dough flour," masa harina is made from dried corn kernels that have been cooked and soaked in alkaline water, which breaks down the corn, increases the nutrient content (most notably calcium), and gives a distinctive taste and character that differs from cornmeal. Used to make tamales, corn tortillas, and chalupas, you can find it in most supermarkets in the international section.

1

2

3

7

8

CALABAZA TAMALES

After soaking the masa harina and letting it cool, combine it with the calabaza pumpkin, Oaxaco cheese, chipotle and jalapeño peppers (photos 1–5). Equally divide the pumpkin mixture among the softened corn husks, leaving a 1-inch border at the tapered end of each husk and around the sides (photos 6–7). Wrap each tamale by bringing in the two long sides and rolling the bundle up. Tie with a strip of corn husk (photos 8–9). Place the tamales in a steamer basket set over a pot of simmering water. Steam for 1 hour, checking the water periodically (photos 10–11). The tamales are done when the husk can be easily peeled away (photos 12–13). Eat and enjoy with friends (photo 14)!

11

12

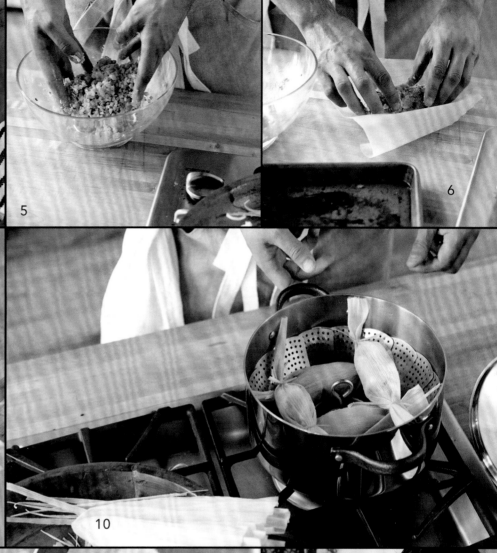

TUNA TARTARE
WITH SMOKY VINAIGRETTE

Angie

SERVES: 2
TIME: 20 MINUTES

1 cup chopped sashimi-grade tuna
2 tablespoons diced red onion
1 tablespoon diced jalapeño
2 sprigs fresh cilantro, chopped
kosher salt
2 tablespoons chipotle chile powder
¼ cup grapeseed oil
½ teaspoon sugar
3 tablespoons fresh lime juice

When Angelo and I taped a segment for my web series "Being Better," he gave me this advice on buying tuna: it should smell like the ocean. Fresh fish should never smell even a little bit fishy. If it does, skip it. When shopping for this raw dish, go with sashimi-quality tuna from a good seafood market and use it that day.

In a medium bowl, combine the tuna, onion, jalapeño, cilantro, and salt to taste. Mix and chill for 10 minutes.

Combine the chipotle powder, oil, ½ teaspoon salt, the sugar and lime juice in a blender and blend on high for 30 seconds. Chill for 10 minutes.

To serve, drizzle the tuna with the vinaigrette and toss.

TOMATO TARTARE
WITH CHIPOTLE & CAPERS

Angelo

SERVES: 4
TIME: 10 MINUTES

4 large vine-ripened tomatoes, finely chopped
2 tablespoons capers, rinsed
3 tablespoons olive oil
2 tablespoons fresh lime juice
½ teaspoon chipotle chile powder
1 allspice berry
¼ teaspoon cumin seeds
1 teaspoon kosher salt
2 sprigs fresh basil

I love a good steak tartare, but I know raw meat is not for everyone. This is a vegetarian riff on the classic using diced tomatoes. Tomatoes aren't going to replicate the flavor and texture of meat, but they're much lighter and full of antioxidants, and have a nice savory taste. Choose vine-ripened tomatoes that are free of blemishes and leave out at room temperature. Refrigeration causes them to lose flavor and become mealy.

Place the chopped tomatoes in a medium bowl.

Combine the capers, olive oil, lime juice, chipotle powder, allspice, cumin, and salt in a blender and blend to create a smooth vinaigrette.

Drizzle the vinaigrette over the tomatoes and gently toss. Transfer the tomato tartare to a serving plate.

Pick the leaves from the basil, roll them up and cut into thin ribbons. Sprinkle over the tartare and serve.

CRISPY TOSTONES

Angie

When I was seven or eight, I used to love to sit in my grandmother's kitchen in Washington Heights and watch her prepare *tostones*, or double-fried plantain chips. She'd first slice up the plantains and deep-fry them in oil before squishing them and frying them again. I still remember her kitchen being littered with brown paper bags, which she used after the first fry to absorb the oil. You could see all the round grease spots, but I didn't care because her tostones were so good! In this recipe, Angelo eliminated the first fry, turning the chips into a lighter snack that's every bit as tasty as my grandmother's.

SERVES: 4
TIME: 20 MINUTES

2 green plantains, peeled
   (see Tip)
grapeseed oil, for frying
1 fresh bay leaf
2 cloves garlic, smashed
kosher salt

Using a sharp knife, cut the plantains lengthwise into long thin slices, about ⅛ inch thick. Place on paper towels and pat dry.

Pour enough oil into a large pot to come about 3 inches up the sides. Clip a deep-fry thermometer on the pot, turn the heat to high, and bring the oil to 325°F. Meanwhile, line a sheet pan with paper towels and put it next to the stovetop.

When the oil is ready, carefully place the plantains in the oil and fry until golden and crispy, 4 to 6 minutes total. Using a slotted spoon, transfer to the prepared sheet pan to drain.

Transfer the plantains to a medium bowl. Break up the bay leaf into small pieces and gently toss with the plantains, rubbing the leaves onto the chips. Add the garlic and salt to taste, and toss again.

Transfer the tostones to a serving dish and serve immediately.

Tip HOW TO PEEL A PLANTAIN *Although the natural inclination is to peel plantains like bananas, you'll quickly find that method won't work. The best way to remove the tough peels is to first cut off the ends of the plantain. Make several incisions down the length of the plantain, without cutting into the fruit, and peel off the sections with your hands.*

SHRIMP & AVOCADO CEVICHE
WITH LIME CREMA

Angie

I love avocados. They are such a great food and don't deserve the bad rap they sometimes get. Okay, they have a high amount of fat, but they're rich in monounsaturated fat—the kind that helps lower your cholesterol—and other nutrients like folate and vitamins C, E, and K. Nutrition aside, I really love how the creamy cubes of avocado mellow out the citrus juices in this dish.

SERVES: 4 TO 6
TIME: 30 MINUTES

1 pound medium shrimp
  (see Tip), peeled, deveined,
  and split in half
¼ cup fresh orange juice
3 tablespoons fresh lime juice
1 tablespoon yuzu juice
  (see page 35)
2 tablespoons sugar
¼ teaspoon kosher salt
2 tablespoons Mexican crema
  (see below)
1 teaspoon grated fresh ginger
½ ripe avocado, peeled and
  cut into chunks
2 teaspoons diced red onion
1 teaspoon chopped jalapeño

WHAT IS MEXICAN CREMA?

Rich and tangy, Mexican crema is similar to French crème fraîche. It has a thinner consistency and softer flavor than sour cream. You can find it in Latin markets or in specialty stores.

Put a bowl of ice nearby. In a medium pot, bring 6 cups water to a boil. Drop in the shrimp and cook only until they just begin to turn pink, about 15 seconds. (Do not overcook.) Remove from the heat, drain, and chill the shrimp on ice.

In a small bowl, combine the orange, lime, and yuzu juices with the sugar, salt, crema, and ginger. Mix well and pour over the shrimp. Chill for 15 minutes. Just before serving, gently toss in the avocado, onion, and jalapeño.

Tip BUYING SHRIMP *No matter the color, fresh shrimp should always feel firm (or look plump) and smell fresh. Because most shrimp are frozen and then defrosted in supermarkets, there's really no point in buying "fresh" shrimp that may be wilting in the displays. Your best bet is to buy bagged frozen shrimp with "IQF" (individually quick-frozen) noted on the label, and then defrost them at home. To thaw, place shrimp in the refrigerator overnight or remove the shrimp from the packaging and place in a bowl in the sink. Let cold water run onto the shrimp for about 15 minutes.*

SHRIMP & PAPAYA CEVICHE

Angelo

Ceviche is a type of dish that entails "cooking" small cubes or thin slices of raw fish in citrus juice. The high level of acidity in the juice changes the protein in the fish, making it opaque and firm. In this dish, I use shrimp for its sweet flavor and succulence, but pre-cook it to cut down on the time it needs to "cook" in the citrus juice. The addition of sweet papaya brings vibrant color, a nice musky flavor, and vitamins A and C.

SERVES: 4 TO 6
TIME: 20 MINUTES

1 fresh bay leaf
1⅛ teaspoons kosher salt
1 pound medium shrimp (see Tip, page 33), peeled and deveined
3 tablespoons fresh lime juice
2 tablespoons yuzu juice (see below)
2 tablespoons sugar
1 ripe papaya, peeled, seeded, and cut into small chunks
1 tablespoon diced red onion
1 tablespoon minced jalapeño

Have a bowl of ice nearby. Mix 6 cups water, the bay leaf, and 1 teaspoon of salt in a large pot. Bring to a boil and add the shrimp. Cook only until the shrimp just begin to turn pink, about 15 seconds. (It is crucial that you don't overcook them.) Remove from the heat, drain, and chill on ice.

In a medium bowl, combine the lime and yuzu juices, sugar, and remaining ⅛ teaspoon salt. Gently mix until the sugar and salt are dissolved. Add the shrimp, papaya, onion, and jalapeño. Gently toss and serve.

WHAT IS YUZU?

Yuzu is a Japanese citrus fruit that resembles a yellow grapefruit. It's about the size of a tangerine, has a bumpy rind, and is quite aromatic. I love its fragrant, tangy flavor, and using it for salads and ceviches. Yuzu can be tough to find, but some Asian markets carry it. You can also order it online or simply buy the bottled juice. Lemon juice is a perfectly good substitute.

TUNA CEVICHE
WITH HEARTS OF PALM & CAPERS

Angelo

Hearts of palm add a delicate and subtle sweetness to this assertively flavored ceviche. Hearts of palm come from the inner core of the cabbage palm tree and are low in fat, cholesterol free, and a good source of fiber. Find them canned or packed in glass jars at most supermarkets.

SERVES: 2 TO 4
TIME: 10 MINUTES

1 cup chopped sashimi-grade tuna
3 tablespoons fresh lime juice
2 tablespoons yuzu juice (see page 35)
3 tablespoons fresh orange juice
½ cinnamon stick, grated, or to taste
2 teaspoons sugar
1 teaspoon diced red onion
1 teaspoon finely diced jalapeño
1 teaspoon chopped fresh cilantro
½ teaspoon kosher salt
3 tablespoons thinly sliced hearts of palm
2 teaspoons capers, rinsed

In a small bowl, combine the tuna with the lime, yuzu, and orange juices, and the cinnamon.

Add the remaining ingredients and toss to combine. Chill in the refrigerator for at least 10 minutes.

Serve the ceviche by itself or wrapped in lettuce leaves.

CHARRED CORN TORTILLAS

Angelo

There's no doubt that fresh corn tortillas taste better than the store-bought varieties, so why not make them at home? Here's a simple recipe I devised. You can form the tortillas by hand or with a rolling pin, but I think it's much easier to use a tortilla press (see Tip). You can also get the kids involved by asking them to roll out the balls of masa and flatten them in the press. They'll be amazed at what those little balls turn into! These go with just about any recipe in this chapter.

SERVES: 8 TO 9
TIME: 25 MINUTES

2 cups instant masa harina (preferably Maseca brand), plus more if needed (see page 27)
½ teaspoon kosher salt
vegetable oil

In a medium bowl, whisk together the masa harina and salt. Pour 1½ cups water over the corn flour mixture and stir. When the water is fully incorporated, begin to knead the mixture in the bowl. After 10 minutes, the dough should feel firm and springy and look slightly dry. Add more water if the dough is too crumbly or a little more masa if the dough is too wet.

Measure 1 heaping tablespoon of dough and roll it into a ball. Flatten the ball on a 6- to 8-inch tortilla press lined with plastic wrap. Remove the tortilla and repeat, shaping 16 to 18 tortillas total. Separate each tortilla with a layer of wax of paper to prevent sticking. If you don't have a tortilla press, place the balls of dough in between pieces of wax paper, and flatten and shape with a rolling pin to a ⅛-inch thickness.

Heat a large cast-iron skillet over medium-high heat. Lightly brush the surface with oil and cook the tortillas one at a time. Within 1 to 2 minutes, the tortilla should begin to char in spots and the edges will start to curl. Flip over and cook on the other side for about 15 seconds. Transfer to a clean kitchen towel and fold it over to keep the tortilla warm. Repeat until all the tortillas are cooked.

Tip SELECTING A TORTILLA PRESS *Though not totally necessary, tortilla presses make forming the tortilla rounds much easier. They come in various sizes and are made out of materials such as wood, cast iron, or aluminum. For this recipe, I prefer a 6- to 8-inch press in any material. You can buy presses at Mexican markets or order them online at Amazon.com.*

BRAISED CABBAGE
& TOMATOES

Angelo

Cabbage is such a versatile vegetable. It can be steamed, boiled, stuffed, sautéed, or braised, as in this recipe. Braising is a technique that entails cooking in liquid for a long period of time. This slow-cooking method is used frequently for meat, but it's also great for vegetables. The cabbage in this dish softens, becomes sweeter, and melds with the other ingredients as it cooks to become a truly delectable side dish.

SERVES: 2 TO 4
TIME: 1 HOUR 10 MINUTES

3 tablespoons olive oil
3 tablespoons chopped onions
1 tablespoon chopped garlic
6 allspice berries
4 whole cloves
1 cinnamon stick
¼ medium head cabbage, leaves roughly chopped
4 vine-ripened tomatoes, cut in half
2 cups crushed canned tomatoes
3 tablespoons sugar
4 sprigs fresh thyme
1 fresh or dried bay leaf
kosher salt

In a medium pot, heat the olive oil over medium-high heat. Add the onions and garlic and sweat until transparent, 3 to 5 minutes. Add the allspice, cloves, and cinnamon stick and cook until aromatic, 2 to 3 minutes. Add the cabbage leaves and fresh tomato halves and cook until the cabbage is slightly tender, 10 to 15 minutes.

Deglaze the pan with the crushed tomatoes and 2 cups water. Add the sugar, thyme, and bay leaf and cook on low heat for 45 minutes until the mixture is stew-like. Season with salt and serve.

Nutritional Note ✳ *Along with kale, Brussels sprouts, broccoli, and cauliflower, cabbage is a member of the cruciferous family of vegetables. Nutrients in cruciferous vegetables may help prevent certain cancers like colorectal or prostate. To select cabbage, look for well-formed heads that are heavy for their size.*

ROASTED SPICED SWEET POTATOES

Angelo

Bring excitement to your dinner table with these brightly colored gems, brimming with vitamins A and C, potassium, and fiber. Though sweet potatoes are great on their own, I amplified their naturally sweet flavor with some of my favorite spices and maple syrup. These are so sweet and delicious that they can be served for dessert with a modest dollop of whipped cream. Leave the spices on top of the potatoes for a rustic look.

SERVES: 4
TIME: 1 HOUR 10 MINUTES

4 medium sweet potatoes,
  washed and scrubbed
½ fresh nutmeg
2 cinnamon sticks
4 whole cloves
2 fresh bay leaves
¼ cup maple syrup
¼ cup olive oil, optional
1 teaspoon kosher salt

Preheat the oven to 350°F.

Prepare 4 squares of aluminum foil. Pierce each potato all over with a fork and place on a foil square. Grate the nutmeg over the potatoes. Top each potato with a half stick of cinnamon, 1 clove, and half a bay leaf. Drizzle with the maple syrup and olive oil, if desired, and season with salt.

Wrap and bake until fork tender, 45 to 60 minutes.

"This is a fun dish you can serve around the holidays, or as an easy side dish for a weekday dinner—prepare the potatoes in advance, stick them in the fridge, and bake and serve them later in the week."

Angie

SUMMER CORN SOUP
WITH TOMATO & CHORIZO

Angelo

You don't always have to use a lot of meat to make a big impact on a dish. In this soup, I use a small amount of chorizo, a Spanish pork sausage with a smoky flavor. Because the chorizo is dried and cured, most of the moisture has been drawn out, making its flavor incredibly concentrated. Scatter some on this soup or on scrambled eggs, and remember, a little goes a long way.

SERVES: 4 TO 6
TIME: 40 MINUTES

3 tablespoons olive oil
2 cups fresh corn kernels
¼ cup roughly chopped tomatoes
1 Thai chile pepper, chopped
1 tablespoon chopped garlic
1 tablespoon minced fresh ginger
1 teaspoon sugar
1 teaspoon kosher salt
3 tablespoons chopped Spanish chorizo

Heat the oil in a large pot over medium heat. When hot, add the corn, tomatoes, chile, garlic, ginger, and sugar and stir constantly for 10 minutes, until all the natural sugars have been released and the mixture is fragrant. Add 4 cups water and cook over low heat for 20 minutes. Transfer to a blender and blend until smooth. Season with the salt.

In a small pan, lightly cook the chorizo for 5 minutes.

To serve, ladle the soup into bowls and garnish with the chorizo.

GREEN PLANTAIN SOUP

Angie

A hearty dish that doesn't have a trace of meat, this soup is made with starchy green plantains, which taste a bit like potatoes here. Not only can you make it a day in advance and let the flavors intensify before serving, but it's supposed to be rustic and chunky so there's no need to blend it. Easy!

SERVES: 2 TO 4
TIME: 40 MINUTES

2 tablespoons olive oil
1 green plantain, peeled and cut into ¼-inch-thick rounds (see Tip, page 32)
2 cloves garlic, smashed
1 medium onion, chopped
½ teaspoon distilled white vinegar
4 sprigs fresh cilantro
2 fresh bay leaves
1 teaspoon coriander seeds
2 teaspoons sesame seeds
kosher salt

Heat the olive oil in a medium sauté pan over medium heat. Add the plantain, garlic, and onion and cook for 5 to 7 minutes, until the onion begins to soften. Add the vinegar, cilantro, bay leaves, and 2 cups water and cook on low heat for 30 minutes, until the plantains are tender.

Meanwhile, using a mortar and pestle, the side of a knife, or a rolling pin, crack the coriander seeds. Toast the sesame seeds in a small dry sauté pan over low heat until light golden brown and fragrant, 3 to 5 minutes.

Season the soup with salt. Garnish with the cracked coriander and toasted sesame seeds and serve.

GARBANZO BEAN & CILANTRO SOUP

 Angelo

Growing up, my tía Carmen was famous for her chickpea salad (Ensalada de Carmen, page 62). To honor her memory, I use chickpeas in this hearty soup that's flavored with smoky chipotle powder and other aromatics. Sprinkle chopped fresh cilantro on top to give color and added freshness.

SERVES: 6
TIME: 2 HOURS

3 tablespoons olive oil
2 tablespoons chopped garlic
3 tablespoons chopped onion
1 tablespoon chopped fresh
   thyme leaves
1 Thai chile pepper, chopped
1 tablespoon chipotle chile
   powder
1 fresh or dried bay leaf
1½ cups dried garbanzo beans
   (chickpeas), soaked overnight
   in water and drained
kosher salt
3 tablespoons chopped fresh
   cilantro

Heat the olive oil in a large pot over medium-high heat. When hot, add the garlic and onion and sweat for 5 to 7 minutes. Add the thyme, chile, chipotle powder, and bay leaf and cook until aromatic, 2 to 3 minutes. Add the chickpeas and 3½ cups water. Bring to a boil, then lower the heat and simmer until the chickpeas are tender, 1 to 1½ hours.

Season with salt and garnish with the cilantro.

Nutritional Note ✳

Chickpeas (or garbanzo beans) are rich in protein, fiber, and iron. Toss them in soups, salads, or stews, or blend them in a food processor to make dips.

SUGARCANE-SKEWERED PORK
WITH PINEAPPLE CHIPOTLE SALSA

— Angelo

In the tropics, you'll often see tall poles of sugarcane, a giant grass that can grow up to twelve feet high. The long, fibrous stalks are used to make cane sugar or byproducts such as molasses, rum, and cachaça (a distilled spirit popular throughout Latin America). In the Dominican Republic, we used to get short stalks of sugarcane and chew on them to extract their sweet juices. In this recipe, I use them to skewer lean cubes of pork for grilling. During cooking, the sugar in the stalks drips onto the pork and caramelizes, creating a delectable treat.

SERVES: 6 TO 8
TIME: 15 MINUTES

vegetable oil, for greasing
1½ pounds pork tenderloin,
   cut into 1-inch cubes
12 to 16 (4-inch-long)
   sugarcane skewers
1 teaspoon kosher salt
½ cup diced fresh pineapple
   (see Tip, page 57)
1 tablespoon minced jalapeño
½ tablespoon minced red
   onion
1 tablespoon chopped fresh
   cilantro
2 tablespoons fresh lime juice
½ tablespoon finely chopped
   chipotle in adobe

Preheat a grill or grill pan to high heat. Lightly grease the grill with vegetable oil.

Thread the cubes of pork onto the skewers and season with the salt. Grill the pork, turning occasionally, until cooked through and slightly charred, about 10 minutes.

Meanwhile, in a small bowl, combine the remaining ingredients.

Arrange the grilled pork on a platter and serve with the salsa on the side.

Tip SOURCING SUGARCANE SKEWERS *Look for sugarcane in the frozen food section of Latin markets and specialty food stores. You can also order them online from melissas.com or kalustyans.com. Still can't find them? Substitute bamboo skewers soaked for at least 30 minutes in a simple syrup made from equal parts water and agave syrup.*

SUMMER CORN FRICASSEE

Angie

Although I certainly didn't grow up next to a cornfield, I love corn as much as Angelo does, and it goes with just about everything. In this recipe, we take corn kernels and sauté them with delish ingredients such as garlic, ham, ripe tomato, and bell pepper. This is so good and, believe me, a snap to make.

SERVES: 6 TO 8
TIME: 30 MINUTES

10 ears of fresh corn, shucked
¼ cup olive oil
¼ cup diced lean ham
1 onion, chopped
2 cloves garlic, chopped
¼ cup fresh cilantro stems
½ green bell pepper, seeded
  and chopped
¼ cup chopped fresh tomato
2 Thai chile peppers, chopped
2 tablespoons white vinegar
kosher salt

Using a sharp knife, slice the corn kernels off the cob.

Heat the olive oil in a large sauté pan over medium heat. Add the corn and lightly sauté for 1 minute. Add the ham and cook for 5 minutes, stirring occasionally, then add the onion and garlic and cook until aromatic. Add the cilantro, bell pepper, tomato, chiles and vinegar and cook for 10 minutes more, or until the sauce lightly glazes the corn. Season with salt and serve.

MANGU MASHED GREEN BANANAS

Angelo

This is a simpler version of my Dominican Mangu (page 115); I wanted to highlight the beauty of the mashed unripe plantains without too many additional ingredients. Our family secret to getting the mangu extra soft is to use cold water. I'm not sure why it works, but my tía Carmen always insisted on it, so that's what I do. I like to eat this just so, or with grilled meat or fish.

SERVES: 4
TIME: 35 MINUTES

6 green plantains, peeled
  (see Tip, page 32) and cut
  in half
kosher salt
¼ cup chopped onion
1 tablespoon white vinegar
¼ cup olive oil
1 tablespoon sugar

Place the plantains in a large pot, cover with 4 cups water, and add 2 teaspoons salt. Bring the water to a boil and cook until the plantains are tender, about 10 minutes. Drain and set the plantains aside.

In a small bowl, combine the onion and vinegar. Let sit for 5 minutes. In a small sauté pan over medium-high heat, heat 1 teaspoon of the olive oil. Add the onions with the vinegar and cook until softened, about 5 minutes. Add the sugar and season with salt.

Mash the plantains with a fork or a potato masher. Add the remaining olive oil and 1 cup cold water and keep mashing until the consistency is very smooth. Serve the mashed plantains with the sautéed onions on top.

YUCCA & PLANTAIN MOFONGO

— Angie

Angelo may have grown up in the country, but I grew up in New York City, where there isn't a whole lot of green spaces and farms. Bodegas were the place to go for getting fruits and vegetables like plantains and yucca—the key ingredients in this version of *mofongo*. Usually made with fried plantains, I love how Angelo changed it up by adding yucca—and steamed it instead of frying, which saves us a ton of calories and fat. Serve with sunny-side up eggs or rice and beans.

SERVES: 4 TO 6
TIME: 20 MINUTES

2 green plantains, peeled (see Tip, page 32) and sliced into ½-inch rounds
1 (4-inch) piece of yucca (see below), peeled and cut into ½-inch chunks
3 tablespoons olive oil
3 cloves garlic, minced
¼ cup minced onion
1 Thai chile pepper, chopped
kosher salt

WHAT IS YUCCA?

Also known as cassava, yucca is a tropical root vegetable that's high in carbohydrates. Because of its high starch content, it can be roasted, boiled, or fried and used as a substitute for potatoes. It's naturally fat free and an excellent source of vitamin C. Store yucca for up to a week in a cool, dry, dark place.

Add 2 inches of water to a medium pot fitted with a steamer basket and bring to a boil. Place the plantains and yucca in the steam basket and steam until tender, 20 to 30 minutes. Remove from the heat.

Heat the olive oil in a small sauté pan over medium heat. Add the garlic, onion, and chile and cook until soft, about 5 minutes. Remove from the heat.

Transfer the plantains, yucca, garlic, onion, and chile to a large mortar. With a pestle, mash until smooth. Season with salt. As an alternative, mash the mixture in a large bowl with a potato masher.

Nutritional Note *To maximize the retention of nutrients during cooking, opt for steaming rather than boiling root vegetables. This helps them retain important water-soluble vitamins that would otherwise leach out into the water when boiled.*

MI ABUELA'S STRING BEANS

Angelo

Mildly flavored green beans are such a great accompaniment with meat, fish, or pretty much anything else. This is my grandmother's go-to recipe that my father frequently made at home. I've embellished it with a few things like Thai chile, but it's basically the same dish I had when I was nine.

SERVES: 4
TIME: 20 MINUTES

¼ cup olive oil
2 pounds string beans, stemmed
⅓ cup tomato paste
1 teaspoon red wine vinegar
2 cloves garlic, smashed
¼ cup chopped onion
1 Thai chile, finely chopped
1 fresh or dried bay leaf
kosher salt

Heat the olive oil in a medium pan over medium heat. Add the beans, stir to coat in the oil, and cook for 5 minutes.

In a small bowl, dissolve the tomato paste in 1 cup water, then pour the mixture into the pan. Stir in the remaining ingredients, season with salt, bring to a boil, then lower the heat.

Cover and simmer until the beans are slightly tender, 10 to 12 minutes. Season with more salt, if necessary, and serve.

Nutritional Note ✳ *String beans are a good source of fiber and vitamin C.*

STEWED OKRA À LA CUBANA

Angelo

Okra is a prickly green vegetable widely used throughout Latin America. It's low in calories and packed with nutrients such as vitamin C, calcium, and magnesium. And it's distinguished by its fiber-rich, seed-filled pods, which naturally release a gooey substance that can be used to thicken soups, stews, and drinks. I like this dish to be a little less gelatinous, so I use a technique that I learned from my tía Carmen to rid the pods of their sliminess.

SERVES: 4
TIME: 30 MINUTES

2½ pounds okra
juice from 2 limes
kosher salt
¼ cup grapeseed oil
1 medium onion, chopped
2 cloves garlic, chopped
1½ pounds vine-ripened tomatoes, roughly chopped
1 medium green bell pepper, seeded and roughly chopped
1½ teaspoons white vinegar
1 fresh or dried bay leaf
2 sprigs fresh thyme
1 yellow plantain

Cut the okra in half lengthwise and place in a large bowl. Add the lime juice and 1½ teaspoons salt. Let sit for 10 minutes to remove the sliminess from the okra. Rinse under cold water.

Heat the oil in a medium pot over medium heat. When hot, add the onion and sauté until softened, 5 to 7 minutes. Add the garlic and stir for another minute, then add the tomatoes, bell pepper, vinegar, bay leaf, and thyme. Cook for 5 minutes.

Peel the plantain as per the Tip on page 32 and slice. Add to the pot with 1½ cups of water and the rinsed okra. Bring to a boil, then reduce the heat and simmer until the plantain and okra are tender, about 10 minutes. Season with salt and serve.

SWEET POTATO & CORN CAKE

Angie

I love sweet potatoes and cornbread, so obviously I'm crazy about this recipe. Cornbread isn't the healthiest of foods, so Angelo added super-healthy sweet potatoes to deliver vitamins A and C, potassium, and fiber to this dish. Steaming (instead of boiling) the potatoes helps keep some of their important nutrients. We also replaced half of the sugar with agave syrup to give it an extra Latin spin. Serve with a piece of fish or chicken, or next to a salad.

SERVES: 12

TIME: 1 HOUR 25 MINUTES

2 medium sweet potatoes
3 cups cornmeal
1 cup all-purpose flour
4 teaspoons baking powder
¼ teaspoon kosher salt
1 cup (2 sticks) butter, melted
½ cup sugar
½ cup agave nectar
4 large eggs
¼ cup diced jalapeño
½ cup shredded Cheddar cheese
½ cup shredded Oaxaca cheese (see page 27)

Peel and cube the sweet potatoes and place them in a steamer basket. Place the basket in a large pot over simmering water. (The potatoes should not touch the water.) Steam for 20 minutes or until tender. Alternatively, pierce the whole potatoes with a fork or knife and place in a microwave-safe bowl. Cover tightly with plastic wrap and microwave on full power for 10 minutes total. Start checking the potatoes after 5 minutes. Rotate and keep cooking in 1-minute intervals. When soft, remove the flesh with a large spoon. In a medium bowl, mash the potatoes with a fork. Let cool.

Meanwhile, preheat the oven to 350°F and lightly grease a 9 x 13-inch baking pan.

In a medium bowl, whisk together the cornmeal, flour, baking powder, and salt. Set aside. In a large bowl, using an electric mixer, cream the butter and sugar until light and fluffy. Add the agave and beat in the eggs, one at a time. Add the mashed sweet potatoes and mix until well incorporated. Add the dry ingredients and mix well. Fold in the jalapeño and both cheeses.

Pour the batter into the prepared pan and bake until a toothpick inserted into the center comes out clean, about 45 minutes.

Nutritional Note ✱ *Microwaving might seem like an unnatural way of cooking, but it can actually preserve more nutrients in foods, such as vitamin C, than other cooking methods. This is partly because food cooks more quickly in the microwave, leaving less time for the vitamins and minerals to break down. And because microwaving requires less water than other methods, there's less opportunity for nutrients to leach out into the water.*

CORN DUMPLINGS
WITH OAXACA CHEESE

Angelo

At my New York City tequileria, Añejo, we normally fry these little balls of goodness. To keep these dumplings leaner, here, I simmer them in broth. This recipe is so easy that I'm excited to make it with my son, Jacob. Kids will enjoy cooking this side dish as much as they enjoy eating it. Serve the dumplings in lettuce leaves with Charred Tomato and Green Olive Salsa (page 141) or Charred Tomato Mole (page 129).

SERVES: 4 TO 6
TIME: 1 HOUR 15 MINUTES

2 tablespoons olive oil
1 tablespoon chopped onion
1 teaspoon chopped garlic
2 cups masa harina (see page 27)
¼ cup fresh or frozen corn kernels
3 tablespoons grated Oaxaca cheese (see page 27)
1 teaspoon chopped chipotle in adobe
½ teaspoon chopped fresh thyme leaves
3½ cups chicken stock

Heat the oil in a small sauté pan over medium-high heat. When hot, add the onion and garlic and cook until transparent and tender, 3 to 5 minutes. Transfer to a medium bowl. Stir in the masa harina, corn, cheese, chipotle, and thyme. Slowly add 1½ cups of the chicken stock, stirring to create a thick paste. Chill for at least 30 minutes.

Take 1 tablespoon of the masa mixture and roll into a small ball. Repeat with the remaining mixture. Chill for 10 minutes.

Heat the remaining 2 cups chicken stock in a medium saucepan over medium-high heat. When it begins to simmer, add the dumplings and cook until they rise to the top of the pot, 5 to 7 minutes. Use a slotted spoon to remove them from the liquid. (You can also serve the dumplings with the broth to make a soup.)

COCONUT-CORN PANCAKES

Angie

My son, Niko, loves spending time in the kitchen with me. He's a really sweet kid who's always excited to cook. It gives him a sense of accomplishment, and I like it because cooking makes him willing to try new foods. Niko has already mastered French toast, and I can't wait until he serves me these pancakes, made with one of my favorite foods—corn.

SERVES: 4
TIME: 30 MINUTES

2 ears fresh corn, shucked
½ cup sweetened coconut
    flakes
3 large eggs, beaten
3 tablespoons sugar
½ cup grapeseed oil
1 cup reduced-fat (2%) milk
2 cups all-purpose flour
1 teaspoon kosher salt
vegetable oil
confectioners' sugar,
    optional
mixed berries, to serve
maple syrup, for serving

Grate the ears of corn against the large holes of a box grater. Alternatively, use a knife to remove the kernels from the cob. You should get about 2 cups.

In a large bowl, combine the corn, coconut flakes, and eggs and mix well. Add the sugar, oil, milk, flour, and salt and stir to combine.

Warm a little vegetable oil in a medium sauté pan over medium heat and pour in the batter, using ¼ cup for each pancake. Cook until golden brown, about 3 minutes per side. Keep warm in a 200°F oven while you repeat with the remaining batter to make 6 to 8 pancakes.

Dust with some confectioners' sugar if you'd like, and serve with mixed berries and maple syrup.

SALADS

Ensaladas

We know the standard green salad isn't much to write home about. But salad can be so much more than lettuce, tomato, and cucumber! In this chapter, we set out to show just how exciting a salad can be when you use ingredients with the right combination of flavors and textures. These recipes are vibrantly colored, incredibly satisfying, and capture the flair and excitement of fresh Latin American ingredients. Most can be served as stand-alone meals, but they also go well with the main dishes in Chapter 4.

CUCUMBER & SERRANO CHILE SALAD

Angelo

Though the true inspiration for this dish comes from Malaysia, I've added the Latin ingredient pineapple. The symbol of hospitality, pineapples originated in South America, but spread throughout Central America and the Caribbean. In this recipe, I love how the crunch and cool flavor of the cucumber marries with the intense heat of the chile and the sweetness of the pineapple. This salad is so refreshing and makes for a great accompaniment to any meal.

SERVES: 4
TIME: 5 MINUTES

2 large cucumbers, halved lengthwise, seeded, and cut into bite-size pieces
1 serrano chile pepper, seeded and minced
½ medium red onion, cut in half and sliced into thin half moons
1 cup large cubed pineapple (see Tip)
¼ cup chopped fresh mint, or to taste
juice of 1 lime
1 tablespoon grapeseed oil
1 teaspoon sugar
1 teaspoon kosher salt
freshly ground black pepper

Toss together the cucumbers, chile, onion, pineapple, and mint in a salad bowl. Pour the lime juice and grapeseed oil over the cucumber mixture and toss to combine. Add the sugar, salt, and pepper to taste, and toss gently to combine.

Tip PICKING A PINEAPPLE *Picking the perfect fruits and vegetables can dictate whether a dish will taste just okay or outstanding. For pineapple, you want to select a sweet and juicy fruit that's robust and will burst with flavor. Let your senses lead the way. First, pick up the pineapple. It should not be too firm or too soft. You should almost be able to sink your fingers into the fruit. Next, smell it. It should have a nice, sweet scent. Once at home, let it sit on the counter for a couple of days to let the sugars concentrate—the flavor will become sweeter and more intense.*

JICAMA & WATERMELON SALAD
WITH CUMIN VINAIGRETTE

Angie

Oh my goodness! This is one of my favorite salads. It's super refreshing and so light. I just love how the starchy jicama pairs with the juicy watermelon. In the summertime, there's nothing better than this. It's so flavorful and satisfying that I literally could have it for every meal. If you're looking for new salad ideas, you *have to* try this dish.

SERVES: 4
TIME: 10 MINUTES

1 whole jicama, peeled and cut
 into large cubes
2 cups cubed watermelon
2 tablespoons olive oil
¼ cup fresh lime juice
¼ teaspoon kosher salt
¼ teaspoon ground cumin
¼ teaspoon chipotle chile powder
1 tablespoon capers, rinsed
1 teaspoon fresh thyme leaves

In a salad bowl, combine the jicama and watermelon.

Meanwhile, in blender, combine the remaining ingredients and puree for 30 seconds or until you have a smooth vinaigrette. Toss with the salad and serve.

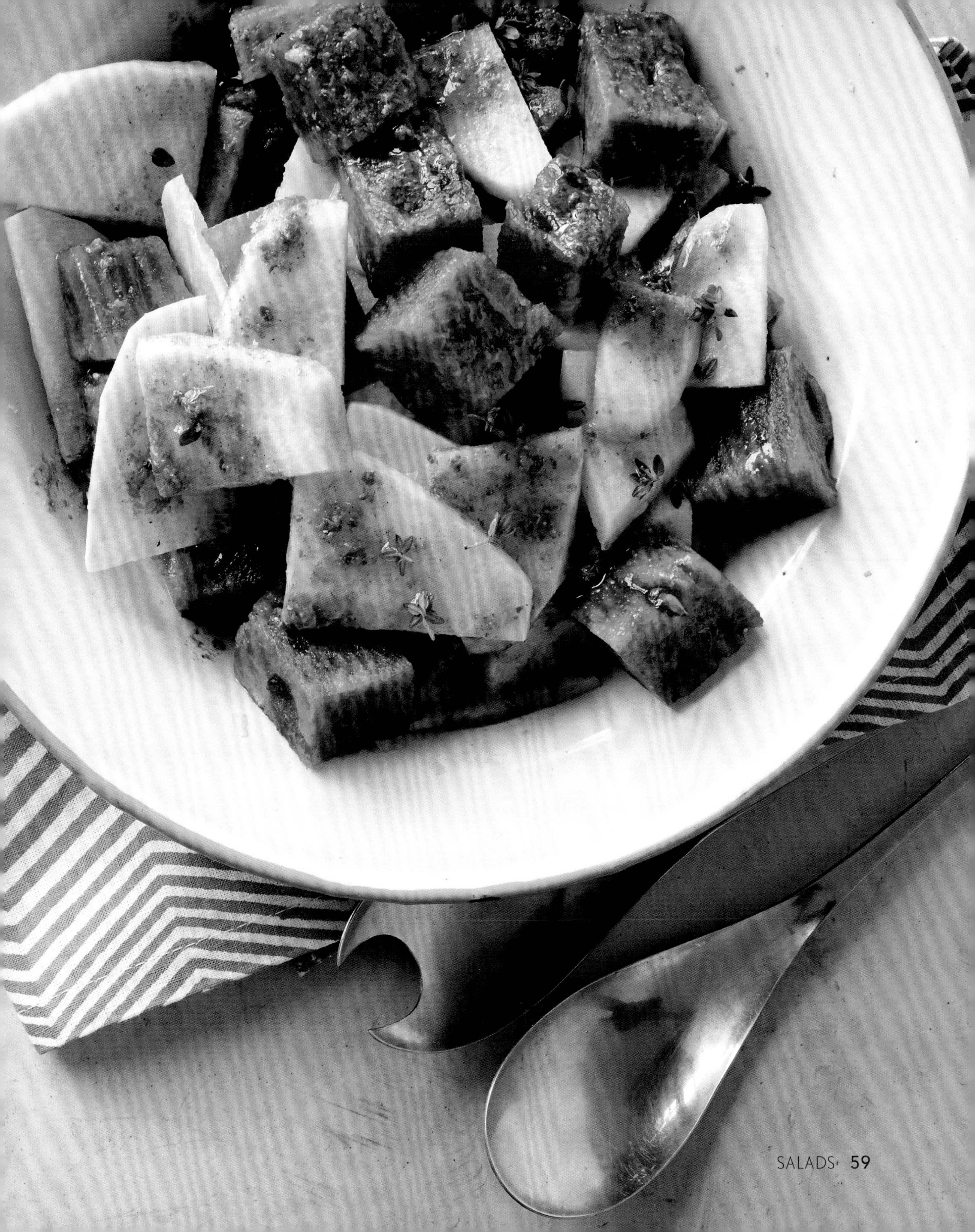

WATERMELON SALAD
WITH GREEN OLIVES & QUESO FRESCO

— Angelo

Have you ever caught a whiff of an old perfume or detergent that brought you back to a specific moment in your life? The scent of these cubed watermelons, briny olives, and salty cheese brings me back to the Dominican shoreline on a hot summer day when I was a kid. I miss those days when I didn't have a care in the world and could spend the whole day frolicking in the sand.

SERVES: 2
TIME: 15 MINUTES

2 cups (½-inch) cubed watermelon
¼ cup pitted green olives
¼ medium red onion, thinly sliced
¼ cup chopped fresh cilantro
2 tablespoons extra-virgin olive oil
1 clove garlic, finely chopped
3 tablespoons lime juice
½ teaspoon kosher salt
3 tablespoons grated queso fresco cheese

In a medium bowl, combine the watermelon with the olives, onion, cilantro, olive oil, garlic, lime juice, and salt. Marinate the salad for 10 minutes to ensure that all the flavors meld.

Transfer the salad to a serving bowl and sprinkle with the queso fresco just before serving.

"Never in a million years would I have thought I'd love watermelon salad, because it sounds so bizarre, but once you go with watermelon in your salad, you can't go back!"

— Angie

CELERY & GREEN OLIVE SALAD
WITH BAY LEAF VINAIGRETTE

Angelo

Bay leaves are one of my most favorite ingredients to use in Latin cooking. The floral flavor is so distinctive and it rounds out any dish. It's often hidden in many recipes so I wanted to bring it to the forefront with this vinaigrette. I prefer fresh bay leaves to extract maximum flavor. You can find them at some well-stocked supermarkets or specialty food stores.

SERVES: 2 TO 4
TIME: 10 MINUTES

BAY LEAF VINAIGRETTE
4 fresh bay leaves, finely
   chopped
3 tablespoons chopped onion
3 tablespoons olive oil
¼ cup red wine vinegar
2 teaspoons sugar
⅛ teaspoon kosher salt

1 cup diced celery
¼ cup green olives, cut in half
1 teaspoon fresh thyme leaves
¼ teaspoon ancho chile
   powder
1 tablespoon finely chopped
   shallots
1 tablespoon chopped fresh
   cilantro

To make the vinaigrette, in a small bowl, combine all of the ingredients and mix well.

In a salad bowl, combine the celery, olives, thyme, chile powder, shallots, and cilantro and mix well. Pour in the vinaigrette, toss to combine, and serve.

ENSALADA DE CARMEN

Angelo

This was part of Tía Carmen's arsenal of dishes she'd make during the summer. It was one of my favorites because it was flavorful and had a hint of Middle Eastern cooking, one of my best-loved cuisines. When the salad was done marinating, she'd serve it in this beautiful old wooden bowl that resembled a wooden canoe, and place it on her flowered tablecloth. You can serve this as is or add cubes of whole-wheat bread to make it a heartier bread salad.

SERVES: 2 TO 4
TIME: 35 MINUTES

2 cups canned chickpeas,
　rinsed and drained
3 tablespoons chopped
　flat-leaf parsley
2 tablespoons chopped
　red onion
3 tablespoons diced tomatoes
1 tablespoon minced jalapeño
2 tablespoons diced red bell
　pepper
3 tablespoons fresh lime juice
2 tablespoons olive oil
1 teaspoon kosher salt
½ teaspoon ground cumin

In a salad bowl, combine all the ingredients. Let sit at room temperature for 30 minutes, mix again, and serve.

Nutritional Note ✳ *Canned beans are handy to keep in the pantry, especially when you need to make something in a pinch, but they can be loaded with sodium. Be sure to rinse and drain the beans before using. This can remove up to 40% of the sodium coating the beans.*

WHAT IS GUAVA PASTE?

Known as *guayabate* or *goiabada*, guava paste is a specialty ingredient popular throughout Latin America that is made by cooking guava fruit with sugar until the mixture becomes a thick puree. When cooled, it has a texture similar to quince paste and a sweet and floral taste. You can find guava paste in wide, flat cans or packaged in plastic at Latin markets, ethnic sections of supermarkets, or online. Alternatively, you can make your own by simply peeling fresh guavas and pureeing them in a food processor. The purée won't be as sweet or concentrated, so adjust the sugar in the recipe accordingly.

THE POSADAS'
MANGO AVOCADO SALAD

— Angie

I'm a huge Yankees fan, and Jorge Posada has always been one of my favorite players. His wife, Laura, runs a program called "Clap for Change!" that empowers families to make positive changes in their lives, including healthy eating. I've made this delicious salad from their cookbook *Fit Home Team* and they were so gracious to let us include it here. It's so good and really easy to put together.

SERVES: 4
TIME: 15 MINUTES

2 ripe mangoes, peeled and
    diced (see Tip, page 150)
½ cup chopped fresh cilantro
¼ cup chopped red onion
¼ cup fresh lime juice
2 ripe Hass avocados, peeled
    and diced
kosher salt and freshly ground
    black pepper

In a salad bowl, carefully fold together the mangoes, cilantro, onion, lime juice, and avocados, being cautious not to mash the ingredients too much, and adding the avocados last so they keep their shape.

Season with salt and pepper and serve.

SWEET & SOUR MANGO GUAVA SALAD

— Angelo

This salad combines a Southeast Asian–inspired harmony of sweet, sour, and salty flavors with two staples of Latin American cuisine, mango and guava. It's awesome with fish, pork, or chicken or even by itself. Be sure to choose ripe mangoes, otherwise the sour flavors will predominate and throw off the balance.

SERVES: 4
TIME: 30 MINUTES

2 ripe mangoes, peeled and
    sliced into ¼-inch pieces
    (see Tip, page 150)
½ teaspoon kosher salt
½ cup fresh or prepared guava
    paste (see left)
3 tablespoons fresh lime juice
1 tablespoon fish sauce
1 tablespoon yuzu juice or
    fresh lemon juice

Place the pieces of mango in a salad bowl and toss with the salt, guava paste, lime juice, fish sauce, and yuzu juice. Chill in the refrigerator for 15 minutes before serving.

ENSALADA DE PULPO

Angelo

The key to preparing octopus is to avoid overcooking it. I like to employ a slow and gentle method to ensure that the octopus stays tender and absorbs the flavors of the cooking liquid. When buying fresh octopus, go to a reputable source such as a fish market or specialty store, and use your nose. Octopus should smell like seawater and nothing else.

SERVES: 4
TIME: 30 MINUTES, PLUS CHILLING

2 lemons, cut in half
1 fresh or dried bay leaf
1 teaspoon kosher salt
1 pound whole octopus
2 tablespoons olive oil

TOMATO VINAIGRETTE
½ cup diced celery
½ cup diced green bell pepper
½ cup chopped vine-ripened
    tomato
1 Thai chile pepper, finely
    chopped
2 teaspoons sugar
¼ teaspoon kosher salt
½ cup red wine vinegar
3 tablespoons olive oil
1 tablespoon chopped flat-leaf
    parsley

Put 2 quarts water in a large saucepan along with the lemons, bay leaf, and salt. Bring to a boil over medium-high heat. Add the octopus, then remove the pan from the heat, letting it rest for 15 to 20 minutes, before placing the pan in the refrigerator to chill for at least 1 hour.

When fully chilled, transfer the octopus to a cutting board. Peel off the outer skin and discard. Cut the octopus into 2-inch pieces.

In a medium-size, deep pan over high heat, add the olive oil. Add the pieces of octopus and cook, turning occasionally, until all sides are golden, 2 to 3 minutes. Remove from the heat.

To make the vinaigrette, in a small bowl, stir all of the ingredients together until the sugar is dissolved.

To serve, fold the octopus into the vinaigrette and transfer to a platter.

AVOCADO & VINE-RIPENED TOMATO SALAD

Angelo

This simple salad showcases my Italian and Dominican backgrounds. It includes staples in the Sosa household—ripe avocados and tomatoes. Practically any day of the week, you'd see some version of this salad on the dinner table. To give it my own spin, I added Thai chile for heat and cinnamon for an earthy tone. If you're scratching your head about the cinnamon, it reacts with the tomato to make it taste even sweeter. Try it and you'll see.

SERVES: 4
TIME: 10 MINUTES

2 ripe avocados
2 medium vine-ripened
   tomatoes, cut into chunks
1 Thai chile pepper, chopped
1 tablespoon capers, rinsed
2 sprigs fresh cilantro,
   chopped
1 cinnamon stick
kosher salt
¼ cup olive oil

With a sharp knife, cut the avocados in half lengthwise and remove the pits. Using a large spoon, remove the flesh from the skins. Place the 4 halves on a platter with the tomatoes. Scatter the chile, capers, and cilantro on top.

Using a microplane, lightly dust the salad with the cinnamon stick. Season with salt, drizzle with the olive oil, and serve.

Nutritional Note ✳ *Rich and creamy, avocados are incredibly healthy and great to have on hand. You might have heard they are high in fat, but they are full of the "good" kind, known as monounsaturated fat—most notably known for its ability to lower cholesterol. Avocados are also packed with vitamins C and E, magnesium, and zinc.*

AVOCADO SALAD
WITH PINEAPPLE LIME VINAIGRETTE

Angie

SERVES: 4
TIME: 20 MINUTES

¼ cup minced pineapple
3 tablespoons lime juice
2 tablespoons sugar
kosher salt
1 teaspoon chopped fresh
   cilantro
2 ripe avocados
⅛ teaspoon ground cumin
⅛ teaspoon chipotle chile
   powder
2 tablespoons olive oil

I'm a salad girl. I love them because they're so light and endlessly versatile. Here's one made from ripe avocados. Simply mix with spices, toss in a light vinaigrette, and serve with grilled fish for an amazing meal.

In a small bowl, combine the pineapple, lime juice, sugar, ⅛ teaspoon salt and the cilantro. Chill in the refrigerator for about 15 minutes.

With a sharp knife, cut the avocados in half lengthwise. Remove the pits and, with a spoon, scrape the flesh into a small bowl. Coarsely cut the avocados and toss with the cumin, chipotle powder, and ⅛ teaspoon salt, then lightly dress with the olive oil.

To serve, plate the seasoned avocados and pour the dressing over.

"This salad is so simple that I plan to make it many more times this summer. It's such a nice accent to a piece of fish or protein. And, as Angelo says, the cinnamon really does bring out the sweetness of ripe tomatoes."

———— *Angie*

AVOCADO & JICAMA SALAD

— Angelo

SERVES: 4 TO 6
TIME: 10 MINUTES

2 ripe avocados
½ cup thinly sliced jicama
¼ cup thinly sliced radish
3 tablespoons hulled pumpkin
  seeds, lightly toasted
¼ cup light sour cream
¼ cup fresh orange juice
2 tablespoon fresh lime juice
3 tablespoons sugar
2 tablespoons olive oil
kosher salt and freshly ground
  black pepper
¼ cup pomegranate seeds

Like varying flavors, an array of different textures can really make a dish come alive. In this recipe, I brought creamy avocado, crisp jicama, crunchy radish, and chewy pumpkin seeds together to create a sensational salad. My mouth is watering right now just thinking about it.

Cut the avocados in half lengthwise and remove the pits. Score the flesh into a cross-hatch pattern and scoop it out using a large spoon. Place the avocados in a medium bowl. Add the jicama, radish, and pumpkin seeds.

In a serving bowl, whisk together the sour cream, orange juice, lime juice, sugar, and olive oil. Transfer the vegetables to the bowl with the dressing and toss well. Season with salt and pepper, garnish with the pomegranate seeds for texture and color, and serve.

AUNT ZUNIA'S
ENSALADA DE REPOLLO

— Angie

SERVES: 8
TIME: 5 MINUTES

½ head (about 1 pound) Napa
  cabbage, very thinly sliced
  (see Note, page 38)
1 radish, very thinly sliced
1 tomato, seeded and thinly
  sliced
¼ papaya, thinly sliced
½ small red onion, thinly sliced
juice of 2 limes
1 cup fresh cilantro leaves
2 tablespoons olive oil
kosher salt
½ cup Cotija cheese, optional
  (see page 27)

In Costa Rica, the expression *pura vida*, or pure life, describes the Tico philosophy of living life to the fullest. My great aunt Zunia, a born and bred Tico (Costa Rican), is a perfect example. She keeps busy taking swim and salsa lessons and making fresh and healthy dishes for the family. This is her favorite Tico recipe, which uses ripe and colorful papaya, a super nutritious fruit packed with vitamins A and C.

In a serving bowl, combine the cabbage, radish, tomato, papaya, onion, lime juice, cilantro and olive oil. Season with salt and gently toss together.

Before serving, sprinkle the cheese on top, if using.

BLACK BEAN & FRISÉE SALAD

FROM ADRIENNE BAILON

Angie

My girl Adrienne is a fellow New Yorker of Puerto Rican and Ecuadorian descent. I've watched her grow up from being a "Cheetah Girl" to the amazing singer-songwriter, actress, dancer, and television personality she is today. Adrienne loves Latin food, but because the camera adds ten pounds, she's changed her eating habits to include lighter fare. This is one of her favorite recipes to keep her looking great on TV and the red carpet.

SERVES: 4
TIME: 15 MINUTES

CUMIN VINAIGRETTE
2 teaspoons toasted whole
　cumin seeds
½ cup red wine vinegar
3 tablespoons olive oil
1 teaspoon fresh thyme leaves
½ teaspoon kosher salt
1 teaspoon sugar

1 head frisée lettuce
2 cups cooked black beans,
　rinsed and drained
2 tablespoons chopped red
　onion
1 tablespoon minced jalapeño
1 ripe avocado, cut into chunks
1 tablespoon chopped fresh
　cilantro
2 strips turkey bacon, cooked
　and chopped into ¼-inch
　pieces

To make the vinaigrette, in a small bowl, combine all of the ingredients. Whisk the mixture well and set aside.

In a large bowl, separate the leaves of the frisée and tear into smaller pieces, if desired. Lightly toss with the beans, onion, jalapeño, avocado, cilantro, and bacon.

Drizzle the vinaigrette over the salad and toss with tongs, being care not to bruise the greens. Serve immediately.

FINGERLING POTATO SALAD
WITH LIGHT HERB MAYONNAISE

Angie

SERVES: 4
TIME: 25 MINUTES, PLUS COOLING

1 pound small fingerling
    potatoes
kosher salt
2 dried or fresh bay leaves
2 sprigs fresh thyme
1 cup light mayonnaise
2 teaspoon red wine vinegar
1 tablespoon chopped fresh
    dill
1 teaspoon fresh thyme leaves
¼ cup chopped ripe avocado
⅛ teaspoon ground cumin

To lighten this salad up, Angelo uses light mayonnaise; I like to use vegan if you could find it. Both have a fraction of the fat and calories in regular mayo and you can barely taste the difference. I also like how he includes chopped avocado in the dressing to add a healthy fat and give a rich and creamy texture.

Place the potatoes, 2 teaspoons salt, the bay leaves and thyme in a medium saucepan and cover with water. Bring to a boil, then simmer on low heat until the potatoes are tender when pierced, 15 to 20 minutes. Drain and discard the bay leaves and thyme.

In a salad bowl, whisk together the mayo, vinegar, herbs, avocado, ¼ teaspoon salt and the cumin. Add the potatoes and gently toss. Cover and refrigerate for 1 hour to cool before serving.

DOMINICAN CHICKEN SALAD

Angelo

SERVES: 6
TIME: 1 HOUR

2 pounds boneless, skinless
    chicken breast
2 sprigs fresh oregano leaves
3 tablespoons white vinegar
2 cloves garlic, chopped
1 tablespoon Worcestershire
    sauce
1 teaspoon kosher salt
1 medium onion, diced
3 tablespoons fresh lime juice
¼ cup olive oil
¼ cup fresh or thawed peas
1 tablespoon capers, rinsed
¼ cup light mayonnaise
3 tablespoons Dijon mustard
¼ cup red seedless grapes, halved
leaves of 6 sprigs fresh
    cilantro, chopped

Deli chicken salad is usually kind of bland and packed with a lot of gut-busting mayonnaise. I took a cue from the Dominicans, who are obsessed with chicken salad, in this lighter and more flavorful version. Serve it in kale or mustard leaves for a light meal.

Cut the chicken into strips, 2½ inches long and 1 inch thick, and place in a medium bowl. Add the oregano, vinegar, garlic, Worcestershire sauce, salt, onion, and lime juice. Toss and let marinate at room temperature for 20 minutes.

Heat the olive oil in a large sauté pan over medium-high heat. Sauté the chicken until cooked and slightly golden on all sides, 5 to 7 minutes. Transfer to a bowl and chill in the refrigerator for 20 minutes.

When you're ready to serve, in a salad bowl, combine the peas, capers, mayonnaise, mustard, and grapes. Fold in the chilled chicken mixture and garnish with the cilantro. To make healthy chicken wraps, scoop the chicken salad into kale or mustard green leaves and roll them up.

MAIN DISHES

Platos Fuertes

We both grew up on Latin dishes that left us feeling heavy and sluggish. In this chapter, we offer light alternatives to the rich meat-and-carb dishes typical of Latin cuisine. Our remixed classics feature leaner cuts of meat, more nutritious sides, and healthier cooking techniques to create mouthwatering, intensely flavored dishes that really hit the spot. We've even thrown in some meatless mains to show just how delicious and filling a plant-based meal can be.

DJ ENUFF'S TURKEY PICADILLO

Angie

I'll let my good friend DJ Enuff, who I worked with for years, do his own intro here: "Angie—or, as my son calls her, Titi Angie—and I have known each other for nearly 20 years and have always been great friends. Over the years we've both dealt with similar weight challenges about how we eat and we've had countless conversations about it. I think everybody is always trying to figure out better ways to eat; even my own family has made a ton of changes in how we prepare our food. We are now very conscious of eating as clean and healthy as possible. This is my easy recipe for Turkey Picadillo, inspired by one that my mom always makes, which uses ground turkey instead of beef. It has all the same flavors of a classic picadillo, but without all the fat."

SERVES: 4
TIME: 1 HOUR

2 medium Yukon Gold potatoes
kosher salt
2 tablespoons olive oil
1 medium onion, minced
1 medium green bell pepper,
   seeded and minced
2 cloves garlic, crushed
1½ pounds lean (90/10)
   ground turkey
2 cups dry red wine
½ pound fresh tomatoes,
   coarsely chopped
⅔ cup pimiento-stuffed green
   olives, drained and chopped
½ cup capers, rinsed
¼ cup golden raisins
1 teaspoon ground cumin
pinch of dried oregano
¼ teaspoon black pepper

Place the potatoes in a large pot with enough water to cover; season with salt. Bring to a boil and then cover and reduce the heat to medium-low. Simmer until the potatoes are tender, about 20 minutes. Drain and let cool.

Heat the olive oil in a large Dutch oven over medium heat. Add the onion, bell pepper, and garlic and cook until softened, about 5 minutes, stirring constantly.

Crumble the ground turkey into the onion mixture, and using a wooden spoon, break the meat into smaller pieces as it begins to cook. Cook until the turkey is completely browned, about 5 minutes. Drain as much fat from the meat as possible.

Stir in the red wine, tomatoes, olives, capers, golden raisins, cumin, oregano, black pepper, and ¼ teaspoon salt. Bring to a boil, then reduce the heat to medium-low. Simmer until the wine reduces and the mixture looks like chili, 8 to 10 minutes.

Peel the cooled potatoes and cut into chunks. Gently fold the cooked potatoes into the simmering beef mixture and cook for 5 minutes more.

"My grandfather always said that you could put whatever you have in your kitchen in picadillo, so we'd always have a mixture of different things like corn, carrots, and raisins. I like olives in mine because it reduces the amount of added salt you'll need."

Angie

TURKEY CHILAQUILES

Angelo

Chilaquiles is a Mexican comfort food made of fried tortilla chips, a red or green sauce, and sometimes meat, typically served for breakfast. Here, I use lean ground turkey and baked tortilla chips to lighten up the meal, and add a few of my own signature touches like capers and fresh thyme.

SERVES: 4 TO 6
TIME: 30 MINUTES

1 pound lean ground turkey
¼ cup olive oil
3 tablespoons chopped onion
1 tablespoon chopped garlic
1½ cups pureed tomatoes
1 tablespoon sugar
3 tablespoons distilled white
   vinegar
1 teaspoon chopped fresh
   thyme leaves
2 tablespoons capers, rinsed
2 cups broken-up baked tortilla
   chips
3 tablespoons low-fat sour
   cream or Mexican crema

In a large sauté pan over medium-high heat, cook the ground turkey in the olive oil. When the meat is golden in color, 5 to 10 minutes, add the onion and garlic. When aromatic, add the tomatoes, sugar, vinegar, thyme, and capers and cook on low heat for 20 minutes, until lightly sauced (the texture should be similar to chili).

Add the chips to the meat mixture and toss well. Top with the sour cream and serve.

ROSIE'S CRISPY CHICKEN THIGHS

Angie

I've known Academy Award–nominated actress Rosie Perez forever. She's Puerto Rican and from New York, so obviously we have to know each other! Seriously though, she's someone I've always admired and through the years has become a great friend. She loves to cook and clearly stays fit. This is a crispy chicken recipe that doesn't use any frying. Here's what Rosie says, "Puerto Ricans don't use batter to fry chicken. We use batter for so many other things, but why not chicken? I don't know, but I'm here to tell you, we make this damn good without it. The problem is we usually use tons of grease to deep-fry it. Here's a solution that produces crispy and delicious chicken."

SERVES: 6
TIME: 40 MINUTES

6 boneless, skin-on chicken thighs
6 sprigs fresh thyme leaves
4 cloves garlic, minced
pinch of cumin, optional
kosher salt and freshly ground black pepper
4 yams, peeled and roughly chopped
2 tablespoons extra-virgin olive oil, plus more for drizzling
2 cups fresh baby spinach

Tip SOME EXTRA HINTS

Do not use white meat. It will dry out. There's no need to cook the spinach, as the heat of the yams and chicken will lightly cook and soften the leaves.

Preheat the oven to 350°F. Add 2 inches of water to a medium pot fitted with a steamer basket and bring to a boil.

Rinse the chicken thighs and pat completely dry. Place on a greased rimmed baking sheet and let sit at room temperature for 15 to 20 minutes.

Season the chicken with the thyme, half of the garlic, the cumin, if desired, and salt and pepper to taste. Scatter over the chicken.

Place the chicken skin-side up in the oven. Bake until light brown and the skin is crispy, about 15 minutes, turning halfway through. Crank up the heat to 500°F and turn the thighs skin-side up and bake until the skin crisps up, 3 to 5 minutes. Keep an eye on the chicken to make sure the chicken skin does not burn. Remove from the oven and tent with a piece of foil.

Meanwhile, steam the yams in the pot until tender, 10 to 15 minutes. Transfer the yams into a bowl. Fold in the remaining garlic and the olive oil and season with a pinch of salt.

Take a spoonful of the yams and place on a plate. Scatter a few spinach leaves over the yams and drizzle with a little olive oil. Top with a chicken thigh. Repeat with the remainder.

RED QUINOA CON POLLO

Angie

It seems like every Latino family has its own version of *arroz con pollo*. But no matter how you make it, traditional rice with chicken is heavy on the carbs. That's why I love Angelo's take on this classic. He's replaced the white rice (and all those empty carbs) with quinoa—a whole grain packed with protein, fiber, and iron. This dish also goes great with Angelo's Ensalada de Carmen (page 62), which adds more protein, vitamins, and minerals. This dish is not totally traditional, but it's close enough to make everyone in my house happy when I serve it.

SERVES: 4
TIME: 50 MINUTES

5 tablespoons olive oil
4 boneless chicken thighs (about 1¼ pounds), cut into 1-inch cubes
kosher salt
1 tablespoon Spanish paprika
¼ teaspoon ground cumin
¼ teaspoon ground turmeric
1 cup chopped Spanish onion
1 tablespoon chopped garlic
1 tablespoon chopped fresh ginger
2 cups dry red quinoa
1¼ cups chopped tomatoes (canned are fine)
1 tablespoon chopped fresh oregano
2 tablespoons chopped fresh cilantro, plus sprigs for garnish
¼ cup pitted green olives

In a large bowl, combine 1 tablespoon of the olive oil with the chicken, ½ teaspoon salt, the paprika, the cumin, and the turmeric. Toss well and let sit at room temperature for 10 minutes.

Meanwhile, heat 2 tablespoons of the olive oil in a medium saucepan over medium-high heat. Add the onion, garlic, and ginger and sweat until aromatic, about 6 minutes. Add the quinoa and stir to combine. Add 2½ cups water and bring to a simmer. Stir in the tomatoes, oregano, and cilantro, then cover. Remove from the heat and let steam undisturbed for 20 minutes.

In a large skillet over medium, heat the remaining 2 tablespoons olive oil. When hot, add the marinated chicken and cook until golden on all sides, 3 to 5 minutes.

To serve, fluff the quinoa with a fork. Season with salt. Transfer to a large platter, top with the chicken, and garnish with the olives and cilantro sprigs.

BROWN RICE PASTELÓN

Angelo

Pastelón is a lasagna-like dish from Puerto Rico that typically uses sliced plantains to replace the pasta layers. In my family we used rice as the starch so that's what I do here. To lighten up this Sosa family favorite and give it a modern spin, I use brown rice and lean ground chicken and turkey. Serve it family style, with a nice salad or a vegetable side.

SERVES: 4 TO 6
TIME: 2 HOURS

2 cups brown rice
¼ cup grated pecorino cheese
2 large eggs, lightly beaten
3 tablespoons grapeseed oil
½ pound lean ground chicken
½ pound lean ground turkey
2 tablespoons chopped onion
2 teaspoons chopped garlic
2 tablespoons finely chopped carrots
1 tablespoon capers, rinsed
1 tablespoon pitted, chopped green olives
1 Thai chile pepper, finely chopped
2 fresh or dried bay leaves
4 sprigs fresh thyme leaves
3 tablespoons distilled white vinegar

In a medium saucepan over medium-high heat, combine the rice with 4 cups water. Cover and bring to a boil. Lower the heat to low and simmer, covered, until the water is absorbed and the rice is tender, about 40 minutes. If it seems too dry or the rice is undercooked, add more water and cook for another 5 minutes. Cover and cool to room temperature. Add the pecorino cheese and eggs to the cooled rice. Mix well and set aside.

In a large sauté pan over medium-high heat, add the oil. Sauté the ground meats until lightly golden, 5 to 10 minutes. Add the onion and garlic and cook for another 5 minutes. Reduce the heat to low, add the carrots, capers, olives, chile, bay leaves, thyme, and vinegar and cook for another 20 minutes. Remove from the heat and let cool.

Preheat the oven to 325°F. Grease a 9 × 13-inch baking dish. Place a third of the rice mixture on the bottom of the dish. Layer with half the meat mixture. Continue alternating layers, finish with the rice mixture on top. Bake until the rice is golden brown, 20 to 25 minutes. (This dish can be refrigerated for 1 to 2 days and reheated in the oven until hot.)

GRILLED CHICKEN
WITH PINEAPPLE JALAPEÑO MARINADE

Angelo

Chicken breasts are a great source of lean protein, but can often become dry and overcooked on the grill. A great trick is to pound the meat into an even layer. This ensures that all parts of the breast finish cooking at the same time, and quickly. I love using pineapple in the marinade. Not only is it indigenous to Latin cuisine, it gives the chicken a nice tropical flavor that goes perfectly with sultry weather.

SERVES: 4
TIME: 1 HOUR

4 boneless, skinless chicken breast halves (about 2 pounds)
½ cup pineapple puree (see Tip, page 126)
1 medium jalapeño, cut in half and seeded
3 tablespoons sugar
1 teaspoon kosher salt
3 tablespoons chopped fresh cilantro
1 teaspoon chopped garlic
3 tablespoons chopped onion
2 sprigs fresh thyme
vegetable oil, for greasing
6 ounces salad greens of choice

Place the chicken breasts in between two pieces of plastic wrap. With a meat mallet or rolling pin, pound to an even $3/4$-inch thickness. Remove the plastic wrap and set the chicken aside in a pie plate or shallow dish.

In a blender, combine the pineapple puree, jalapeño, sugar, salt, cilantro, garlic, onion, and thyme. Blend until smooth, pour over the chicken, and marinate in the refrigerator for 45 minutes.

Preheat an outdoor grill or grill pan to medium-high heat. Using tongs, dip folded paper towels into vegetable oil and rub over the grill. Remove the chicken from the marinade and grill until cooked through, basting with the leftover marinade, 3 to 4 minutes per side. Serve over salad greens.

POLLO GUISADO
FROM ROBINSON CANO

Angie

Former New York Yankee Robinson Cano loves *pollo guisado*. Not only is it a staple from his native Dominican Republic, it's pure Latin comfort food. Traditionally made with whole chicken, Robinson's version is simpler and leaner with chicken breast, a favorite power food among many athletes. It's the perfect dish for anyone with an active lifestyle.

SERVES: 4
TIME: 1 HOUR

1 pound boneless, skinless chicken breast, cut into 2½-inch-long strips
2 medium green bell peppers, seeded and thinly sliced
1 small red onion, thinly sliced
4 plum tomatoes, cut into quarters
1 large carrot, peeled and roughly chopped
1 medium baking potato, unpeeled, cut into small cubes
¼ cup chopped celery
¼ cup pitted green olives
1 small clove garlic, mashed into a paste (see Tip)
1 teaspoon ground cumin
1 teaspoon chili powder
2 sprigs fresh oregano
2 sprigs fresh thyme
1 dried bay leaf
1 teaspoon agave nectar
1 tablespoon tomato paste
2 lemons, cut in half
kosher salt
2 tablespoons vegetable oil

In a large bowl, combine the chicken strips, vegetables, spices, herbs, agave, and tomato paste. Squeeze the juice from the lemons over the chicken mixture and season with a pinch of salt. Toss to combine and marinate at room temperature for at least 30 minutes.

In a large heavy-bottomed saucepan or pot, heat the vegetable oil over medium-high heat. Remove the chicken from the marinade and sear in the pan until browned, 8 to 10 minutes, turning as needed. Reserve the marinade and the vegetables.

When the chicken is seared, add enough water to cover and bring to a boil. Add the reserved marinade and vegetables and cover the pan with a tight-fitting lid. Reduce the heat to low and simmer until all the ingredients are tender and the chicken is cooked through, adding more water if necessary, about 10 minutes. Season with salt. (This stew can be made ahead and kept in a resealable plastic container for 3 to 4 days in the refrigerator. Reheat on the stovetop or microwave until hot.)

Tip HOW TO MASH GARLIC INTO A PASTE *In this dish, I prefer mashed over minced garlic because it provides a more nuanced and rounded flavor. I find the best way to break down garlic is to hit the clove with the flat part of a knife. Sprinkle a little kosher salt over the flattened garlic. (The abrasiveness of the salt will help break down the fibers of the garlic.) Holding the knife at an angle, drag the knife over the garlic and begin to work the garlic in an east-to-west motion. Continue to flatten and mash the garlic until it becomes a paste.*

ORANGE & CILANTRO CHICKEN
FROM HENRY SANTOS

Angie

As a member of the bachata group Aventura, Henry Santos lived many years on the road. He says, "I ended up 40 pounds overweight. There was a point when I knew I had to change, not only for myself, but for my newborn son. I started training and changing the way I ate. I learned to make protein delicious and low in calories with the right seasonings. Everyone loves this dish, and can't believe it's so low in calories."

SERVES: 4
TIME: 25 MINUTES,
PLUS MARINATING

¼ cup finely chopped fresh
    parsley
¼ cup finely chopped fresh
    cilantro
3 cloves garlic, minced
zest and juice of 1 sour orange
    (use 1 orange and 1 lime if
    sour orange is not available)
⅔ teaspoon ground cumin
¼ teaspoon ground coriander
1 Thai chile pepper, finely
    chopped
4 tablespoons grapeseed oil
kosher salt
4 boneless, skinless chicken
    breasts
¼ cup honey

Preheat the oven to 425°F.

In a small bowl, combine the parsley, cilantro, garlic, orange zest, cumin, coriander, chile, 3 tablespoons of the oil, and a pinch of salt.

Sprinkle salt on all sides of the chicken breasts, then place in a resealable bag. Add the herb mixture to the bag and seal, pressing out all the air. Rub the mixture over the chicken through the bag. Let marinate at room temperature for 30 minutes.

In a heavy-bottomed, cast-iron pan, heat the remaining tablespoon oil over medium-high heat. When the oil is hot, add the chicken and cook until browned, about 5 minutes. Transfer the pan to the oven and cook until a meat thermometer inserted into the thickest part of the chicken registers 160°F, about 12 minutes. Transfer the chicken to a platter.

In the same pan over medium heat, add the honey and sour orange (or orange and lime) juice and a dash of salt. Whisk together until well combined. Drizzle the sauce over the chicken breasts and serve.

"Born in the Dominican Republic, Henry is a wildly popular solo artist. Besides being crowned 'King of the Dance Floor' by TV fans, he's also a big foodie and cook. Though he's crazy busy, Henry has joined me in partnering with NY Presbyterian Hospital's CHALK campaign to help combat obesity."

Angie

CELIA CRUZ'S
POLLO GUARACHERO

Angie

I've always felt a connection to the great singer Celia Cruz because she reminds me a lot of my paternal grandmother, who passed away when I was young. I met Celia at a concert years ago and she was so sweet, welcoming, and funny. We took a picture together that night, and, to this day, I keep it in my kitchen. Celia's family says she absolutely loved guava and talked about making this dish often. They were gracious enough to share it with us.

SERVES: 4
TIME: 35 MINUTES

1½ pounds boneless, skinless chicken thighs
1 teaspoon dried oregano
kosher salt
2 large eggs
3 cups breadcrumbs
½ cup guava paste, preferably Goya
3 tablespoons fresh lime juice
1 (1-inch) piece fresh ginger, grated
1 serrano chile pepper, finely chopped
¼ cup cilantro leaves, torn

Preheat the oven to 350°F. Place a cooking rack on a rimmed baking sheet.

Place the chicken in a medium bowl and season with the oregano and salt.

Whisk the eggs in a deep bowl. Place the breadcrumbs on a plate. One by one, coat each thigh in the egg, then coat evenly with the breadcrumbs and place on the prepared baking sheet.

Bake until the chicken is golden brown and an instant-read thermometer inserted into the thickest part of the thighs reaches 165°F, 20 to 25 minutes.

In a small saucepan on medium-low heat, mix together the guava paste, lime juice, ginger, and chile. Whisk to combine and cook for about 2 minutes, or until the guava mixture has loosened slightly and the ingredients are well incorporated.

Toss the chicken in the guava mixture or drizzle the mixture on top of the chicken. Garnish with the cilantro leaves.

CHICKEN ROPA VIEJA

Angelo

The scent of this dish brings me back to my childhood, when cooking brought us all together as a family. I can see myself running around the kitchen and garden with my six siblings in search of ingredients for my dad. Although we're scattered all around the country now, I love how something so simple as the aroma of *ropa vieja* can transport me back thirty years. Traditionally made with beef, I wanted to demonstrate the flexibility of the dish by substituting chicken breast, a much leaner meat.

SERVES: 4
TIME: 40 MINUTES

1½ pounds boneless, skinless chicken breast
1 small red onion, quartered
1 tomato, quartered
1 carrot, peeled and cut into 1-inch pieces
2 cloves garlic, peeled, plus 2 cloves, minced
2 tablespoons olive oil
1 small onion, thinly sliced
½ medium green bell pepper, seeded and thinly sliced
½ medium red bell pepper, seeded and thinly sliced
¼ cup chopped fresh tomatoes or San Marzano canned crushed tomatoes
¼ cup dry white wine
1 teaspoon ground cumin
kosher salt and freshly ground black pepper

In a large pot, place the chicken, red onion, tomato, carrot, and cloves of garlic. Add enough water to cover, then turn the heat to medium-high and bring to a boil. Skim and discard the foam that floats to the surface. Reduce the heat to medium-low and simmer, uncovered, until the chicken is tender, about 10 minutes.

Remove the chicken to a cutting board. When cool enough to handle, shred it with a fork into strips as thick as a pencil; set aside. Strain the cooking liquid and set aside, discarding the vegetables.

Heat the olive oil in a large skillet over medium heat. Add the minced garlic, sliced onion, and bell peppers to the pan and cook until softened, 3 to 4 minutes. Stir in the tomatoes, white wine, cumin, and enough of the reserved broth to create a thin sauce. Simmer for about 5 minutes, then add the shredded chicken. The sauce should lightly coat the meat. Season with salt and pepper and serve.

BEEF ROPA VIEJA

Angelo

This recipe is a quicker adaptation of traditional *ropa vieja*. While there are many theories to explain the name, there's no doubt that the meat is shredded at the end of cooking to resemble rags, hence the translation to "old clothes." Instead of serving this with a carb-heavy side of rice and beans, you can lighten it up by serving it as a "garnish" on a salad composed of beautiful lettuces. And, as a bonus, you don't need to whip up a dressing; simply use the sauce from the meat.

SERVES: 4
TIME: 35 MINUTES

1 tablespoon grapeseed oil
2 pounds beef flank steak, trimmed of fat
1 cup low-sodium beef broth
½ pound fresh tomatoes, roughly chopped
1 small red onion, sliced
1 medium green bell pepper, seeded and sliced into strips
2 cloves garlic, chopped
1 teaspoon ground cumin
2 teaspoons kosher salt
1 teaspoon chopped fresh cilantro
1 tablespoon olive oil
1 tablespoon white vinegar
6 ounces mixed lettuce leaves

Heat the grapeseed oil in a large skillet over medium-high heat. Sear the steak, about 4 minutes per side.

Transfer the beef and juices to a medium-sized, heavy-bottomed pot. Cover with the beef broth and stir in the tomatoes, onion, bell pepper, and garlic with the cumin, salt, cilantro, olive oil, and vinegar. Cook, covered, over medium heat for 45 to 60 minutes, until the meat is tender.

When ready to serve, shred the meat with forks and place atop mixed lettuce leaves.

ARGENTINIAN SKIRT STEAK

— *Angie*

Fat Joe and I go way back. This is one of his favorite recipes and he says, "A lean piece of beef can have less fat and calories than certain parts of poultry. It provides many nutrients that you can't get from any other food and it tastes great. When I enjoy a piece of steak, I like to pair it with fresh vegetables to cut through the richness. Elimination is not a part of my diet."

SERVES: 4
TIME: 15 MINUTES,
PLUS MARINATING

4 (6- to 8-ounce) pieces of skirt
   or flank steak
6 cloves garlic, chopped
1 large red onion, sliced
¼ cup light olive oil
2 tablespoons sugar, optional
3 tablespoons low-sodium soy
   sauce
½ cup cream sherry, preferably
   Harvey's Bristol Cream
fine sea salt and freshly ground
   black pepper
vegetable oil, for greasing

Place the steaks in a large resealable bag.

In a large bowl, whisk the garlic, onion, olive oil, sugar, if using, soy sauce, and sherry together and season with salt and pepper. Pour the marinade into the bag with the steaks and seal. Let sit in the refrigerator for at least 2 hours, preferably overnight.

When ready to cook the steaks, brush an outdoor grill or cast-iron grill pan with vegetable oil and preheat to high (see Tip). Remove the steaks from the marinade and pat dry with paper towels. Discard the marinade.

Cook the steaks for 3 to 5 minutes on each side for medium-rare. Let rest for 5 minutes before slicing on a diagonal across the grain.

Tip GRILLING INSIDE OR OUT *If using an outdoor charcoal or gas grill, let the coals or gas in the grill get completely hot before grilling the steaks. If cooking indoors, use a ridged cast-iron pan for grill marking if you have one, but a regular cast-iron pan or oven broiler will work just as well.*

"I've known Fat Joe since I started in the music business over twenty years ago and he's someone that really takes his health seriously these days. In recent years, he lost eighty pounds through exercise and diet."

— *Angie*

GRILLED SKIRT STEAK TACOS

Angelo

I like using skirt steak as opposed to ground beef in this recipe because it's incredibly flavorful and satisfying. Trust me, there's nothing like biting into a taco filled with slices of spice-rubbed meat with a crispy char on the surface. The lightly pickled vegetables and cilantro add a welcome acidity and brightness to this dish that makes it brilliant.

SERVES: 4
TIME: 30 MINUTES,
PLUS MARINATING

1 tablespoon cumin seeds
1 tablespoon coriander seeds
2 dried bay leaves
kosher salt
½ pound skirt steak
3 tablespoons grapeseed oil
1 cup shredded carrots
1 cup shredded cabbage
¼ cup red wine vinegar
3 tablespoons sugar
1 tablespoon Tabasco sauce
8 (6-inch) corn tortillas
fresh cilantro sprigs

In a small, dry sauté pan over medium heat, lightly toast the cumin, coriander, and bay leaves until aromatic, about 2 minutes. Let cool completely, then grind the spices in a spice grinder with 1 tablespoon of salt until very fine.

Pat the steak dry with paper towels and rub with the oil and the spice mixture until thoroughly coated. (Transfer any extra spice rub to an airtight container and store in a dark place for up to 6 months.) Let the steak stand at room temperature for 30 minutes to marinate.

In a large bowl, combine the carrots, cabbage, and 3 tablespoons salt and let stand for 30 minutes. Rinse the vegetables, squeeze out any excess liquid, and set aside.

Meanwhile, in another large bowl combine the vinegar, sugar, and Tabasco. Add the vegetables to the bowl and toss well.

Heat an outdoor grill or a grill pan to medium-high heat and cook the meat until well charred on the outside but still pink on the inside, about 2 minutes per side. Let rest for a couple minutes before thinly slicing against the grain.

Wrap the tortillas in a damp kitchen towel and steam them in the microwave until soft, 1 minute or less. Using tongs, carefully flash each tortilla over a burner, turning once, to release the corn flavor.

To serve, place a spoonful of the marinated vegetables on each tortilla, top with a few slices of the beef, and garnish with a sprig of cilantro.

CARNE ADOBADA

Angelo

Before I opened my restaurant, Añejo, in New York, I spent a lot of time researching Mexican dishes to really understand the complex flavors and ingredients used in the cuisine. I came across *carne adobada*, a chile-braised pork dish, which is actually New Mexican in origin, but I loved it so much I put it on the menu. This is my version.

SERVES: 4
TIME: 1 HOUR 30 MINUTES,
PLUS MARINATING

2 tablespoons chipotle chile powder
2 teaspoons ground cumin
4 whole cloves
1 teaspoon cayenne pepper
2 teaspoons kosher salt
1 pound boneless pork shoulder
5 tablespoons olive oil
3 tablespoons fresh lime juice
3 tablespoons honey
2 tablespoons white wine vinegar
3 cups chicken stock
lettuce leaves or tortillas, to serve

In a large bowl, stir together the spices and salt. Rub the spice mixture all over the pork and let marinate for 1 hour at room temperature.

Heat the olive oil in a medium pot over medium-high heat. When hot, add the pork and sear on all sides, about 10 minutes total. Add the remaining ingredients and bring to a boil, then lower the heat and simmer for about 1 hour or until an instant-read thermometer inserted into the center of the pork reaches 155° to 165°F.

Remove the pork to a cutting board. Reduce the liquid in the pot until it thickens slightly. Slice the meat and serve with the pan juices in fresh lettuce leaves or tortillas.

ARROZ ATOLLADO

Angie

My friend the amazingly talented actor/comedian John Leguizamo asked his mother to share this recipe for *arroz atollado*, which is served a little more moist than regular rice. This can also be prepared with beef or chicken and with chorizo, too. If using chorizo in addition to a primary protein, add it to the pot at the same time. This is a one-pot meal so all you need is a salad and dessert. As John's mother says, "*Buen provecho!*"

SERVES: A COLOMBIAN ARMY!
TIME: 1 HOUR 30 MINUTES

1 cup extra-virgin olive oil (preferably cold pressed)
6 scallions, finely chopped
5 cloves garlic, finely minced
2 large, ripe tomatoes, finely chopped
3 tablespoons finely chopped chipotle in adobo
5 sprigs fresh cilantro
fine sea salt and freshly ground black pepper
½ teaspoon ground cumin, plus more for seasoning
3 pounds pork ribs, cut into 1½-inch pieces
5 cups dry long-grain rice (preferably Carolina brand)
2 cups fresh or frozen peas
3 medium carrots, minced

Heat the olive oil in a 7-quart pot over medium heat. When hot, add the scallions and garlic and sauté until fragrant, about 5 minutes. Add the tomatoes and chipotle in adobo and cook for 3 minutes. Chop up 4 of the cilantro sprigs, add to the pot, and cook for another 2 to 3 minutes.

Stir in ½ tablespoon salt, ½ tablespoon pepper, and the cumin. Add the pork ribs and brown on all sides, 5 to 7 minutes. Stir in 10 cups of water. Add the rice, peas, and carrots and stir again. Drop in the remaining cilantro sprig.

Cook, covered, over medium heat until most of the water has been absorbed and the rice grains have opened, about 60 minutes. Turn off the heat and leave covered for 10 minutes.

Taste the broth and season with more salt, cumin, and black pepper if necessary.

FISH TACOS
WITH CHUNKY GUACAMOLE & CHIPOTLE SYRUP

— Angie

I truly believe that guacamole should be something you only eat fresh. If you buy it packaged from the store, you really don't know what's in there or how long it's been sitting around. No matter what, homemade is *always* going to be better and you can mix it up with so many variations (see pages 135 to 138). So guys, don't buy pre-made guac, especially for this recipe!

SERVES: 2 TO 4
TIME: 35 MINUTES

CHIPOTLE SYRUP
3 tablespoons agave nectar
1 teaspoon lime juice
2 teaspoons chipotle chile
    powder
¼ cup pineapple juice

CHUNKY GUACAMOLE
2 ripe avocados
2 tablespoons fresh lime juice
2 tablespoons diced fresh
    tomatoes
1 tablespoon minced jalapeño
1 tablespoon red onion
2 teaspoons chopped fresh
    cilantro
½ teaspoon kosher salt

vegetable oil, for greasing
1 pound mahi-mahi fillet, cut
    into 4 pieces
kosher salt
4 (6-inch) corn tortillas
½ cup shredded cabbage
¼ cup grated Cotija cheese
    (see page 27)

To make the chipotle syrup, in a small saucepan over medium heat, combine the ingredients and bring to a boil. Cook until it becomes a thin glaze, about 5 minutes. Set in the fridge to chill.

To make the guacamole, with a sharp knife, cut the avocados in half lengthwise. Remove the pit and, with a spoon, scrape the flesh into a small bowl. Add the remaining guacamole ingredients and mix together with a fork, lightly smashing the avocados. Set aside.

Preheat an outdoor grill or grill pan over high heat. Using tongs, dip folded paper towels into vegetable oil and rub over the grill. Season the fish with salt and cook on both sides until cooked through, 5 to 7 minutes total.

To serve, lightly toast the tortillas on the grill or pan. Layer the tortillas with the cabbage, guacamole, and fish. Sprinkle with the cheese and drizzle the chipotle syrup over the tacos.

FLAKED BACALAO STEW

My tía Carmen made a salted codfish (bacalao) stew with canned tomatoes that was so tasty, I'd ask her to send me back to Connecticut with a container of it so I could enjoy it during the week. I always use fresh produce when I can, because it has a brighter flavor than canned. So this version uses fresh tomatoes. Serve it over brown rice or in crisp lettuce leaves.

SERVES: 4
TIME: 45 MINUTES, PLUS SOAKING

1½ pounds salted codfish
¼ cup olive oil
1 medium onion, thinly sliced
4 cloves garlic, smashed
1½ pounds fresh vine-ripened
   tomatoes, roughly chopped
1 medium green bell pepper,
   chopped
¼ cup chopped fresh cilantro
2 fresh or dried bay leaves
3 tablespoons white vinegar
kosher salt

Soak the salted codfish for 2 to 4 hours in water, then drain.

In a large pot, heat the oil over medium-high heat. When it's hot, add the onion and garlic and cook until slightly softened, 2 to 3 minutes. Reduce the heat to low, add the cod, and cook for about 5 minutes, using a wooden spoon to break the fish up as it cooks.

Add the tomatoes, bell pepper, cilantro, bay leaves, and 1 cup water and cook over low heat for another 15 minutes. If the stew looks too dry, add up to 1 more cup of water.

Add the vinegar and season with salt. Raise the heat to medium-high and bring the mixture to a boil, then reduce the heat and simmer for another 15 minutes, stirring occasionally.

DOMINICAN FISH STEW

Angelo

SERVES: 4
TIME: 20 MINUTES

2 tablespoons olive oil
1 medium onion, chopped
4 cloves garlic, minced
1 pound flaky white fish, cut
   into 1½-inch pieces
1 (14-ounce) can diced
   tomatoes
1 poblano chile pepper,
   chopped
¼ cup chopped fresh cilantro
2 tablespoons sliced pimiento-
   stuffed green olives
1 tablespoon capers, rinsed
1 teaspoon dried oregano
½ teaspoon kosher salt
1 avocado, pitted and
   chopped

Every year around Good Friday, Tía Carmen made this incredible dish as an alternative to eating meat. She always knew how to coax the flavors out of ingredients, and balance the sweetness and acidity in every dish that she made. My aunt served this with white rice but it would be perfect with quinoa or brown rice.

Heat the olive oil in a large, high-sided skillet or Dutch oven over medium heat. Add the onion and cook, stirring occasionally, until softened, about 2 minutes. Add the garlic and cook, stirring, for 1 minute.

Add the fish, tomatoes and their juices, chile, cilantro, olives, capers, oregano, and salt and stir to combine. Add up to ½ cup water if the stew seems dry. Cover and simmer for 10 minutes, until the fish is tender and flakes easily with a fork.

Garnish with the avocado and serve hot or at room temperature.

GRILLED BASS
WITH CORN AND JALAPEÑO SALSA

—— *Angie*

SERVES: 4
TIME: 25 MINUTES

2 tablespoons olive oil
2 cups fresh corn kernels
1 tablespoon minced jalapeño
2 teaspoons minced red onion
2 tablespoons chopped fresh
    tomatoes
1 teaspoon grated fresh
    ginger
2 tablespoons fresh lime juice
2 tablespoons coconut water
½ teaspoon kosher salt
1 teaspoon sugar
vegetable oil, for greasing
4 (5-ounce) black bass fillets
kosher salt

For fish, I like to grill it—it's a fast, easy, and healthy way to cook and leaves the fish with a smoky flavor that just screams summer. In this recipe, Angelo pairs bass with a delish salsa made with corn. In case you didn't know it already, I love corn.

First make the salsa: Heat the olive oil in a medium sauté pan over high heat. When hot, add the corn and char until tender, 2 to 3 minutes. Remove from the heat and cool to room temperature. Stir in the remaining ingredients except the vegetable oil and fish and set aside.

Preheat an outdoor grill or grill pan over high heat. Using tongs, dip folded paper towels into vegetable oil and rub over the grill. Season the fish with salt and cook on both sides until cooked through, 5 to 7 minutes total.

Serve the corn salsa on top of the fish.

BLACK BASS
WITH ORANGES AND ANCHO CHILE OIL

—— *Angelo*

SERVES: 4
TIME: 30 MINUTES

2 navel oranges, segmented
½ Thai chile pepper
2 tablespoons plus ¼ cup
    olive oil
1 tablespoon torn fresh cilantro
1 tablespoon torn fresh basil
1 teaspoon chopped fresh
    thyme
kosher salt
2 tablespoons ancho chile
    powder
1 pound skin-on black bass
    fillets, cut into 4 pieces
3 tablespoons grapeseed oil

Fish and citrus are a classic combination, especially in Latin cuisine. Here I pair seared black bass fillets with bright and juicy orange segments, which are low in calories and a great source of vitamin C.

Place the orange segments in a small bowl with the chile, 2 tablespoons olive oil, the herbs, and ¼ teaspoon salt. Cover and chill in the refrigerator.

In a small saucepan, combine the remaining ¼ cup olive oil with the chile powder and 1 teaspoon salt and stir. Warm on low heat for 5 minutes. Remove from the heat and set aside.

Season both sides of the bass with salt. Heat the grapeseed oil in a medium nonstick sauté pan over high heat. Carefully place the fish skin-side down. Sear until golden brown, 4 to 5 minutes. Gently turn the fish and cook for another 1 to 2 minutes. Transfer the fish to individual plates and garnish with the orange salad. Drizzle with the ancho chile oil and serve.

BANANA LEAF–WRAPPED FISH VERACRUZ

Angelo

SERVES: 2
TIME: 30 MINUTES

2 large pieces banana leaf,
   thawed if frozen and rinsed
1 (2½-pound) whole mahi-
   mahi, cleaned and gutted
kosher salt
2 sprigs fresh thyme, plus
   leaves for garnish
1 fresh or dried bay leaf
2 medium tomatillos, husked,
   rinsed, and chopped
2 medium tomatoes, chopped
1 teaspoon chopped garlic
2 tablespoons capers, rinsed

Imagine you are in Mexico, roasting a bundle of whole fish with aromatics in banana leaves over a fire on the beach. Then use the leaves like a plate and eat the fish with your hands for a delightfully primitive experience. Back in the USA, you can find fresh or frozen banana leaves at Latin markets.

Preheat the oven to 350°F.

Place the banana leaves on a work surface and overlap them to create a wrapper large enough to enclose the fish. Place the fish in the middle of the leaves. Open up the fish and season the cavity with salt, the thyme sprigs, and the bay leaf. Scatter the tomatillos, tomatoes, garlic, and capers on top of the fish and wrap the leaves around, completely encasing it. You may need to use butcher's twine to hold it together.

Place the pouch on a rimmed baking sheet and roast for 25 minutes, or until the fish is tender and cooked through. Garnish with fresh thyme leaves.

COASTAL WHOLE FISH
WITH PINEAPPLE & COCONUT

Angelo

As a young boy while visiting La Romana, a city on the coast of the Dominican Republic, I remember watching the fishermen charcoaling entire fish on banana leaves. This super-healthy grilled bass is enhanced by pineapples and coconut, giving it tropical flavor and sweetness.

SERVES: 2
TIME: 25 MINUTES

1 (2½-pound) whole black
   bass, cleaned and gutted
kosher salt
2 fresh or dried bay leaves
4 sprigs fresh thyme
4 sprigs fresh cilantro
1 Thai chile pepper, chopped
½ cup sweetened coconut
   flakes
½ cup pineapple slices
vegetable oil, for greasing
3 tablespoons olive oil

Preheat an outdoor grill or grill pan over medium-high heat.

Open up the fish and season the cavity with salt, then stuff the cavity with the bay leaves, thyme, cilantro, chile, coconut flakes, and pineapple. Skewer the fish to enclose the ingredients.

Using tongs, dip folded paper towels into vegetable oil and rub over the grill. Drizzle the olive oil over the fish and place on the grill. Cook on one side until grill marks appear and the flesh turns opaque, about 10 minutes. Gently flip the fish and cook for another 10 minutes, until cooked through.

DOMINICAN MANGU

Angelo

One of my fondest memories of visiting relatives in the Dominican Republic as a child is sharing this simple, yet magical, dish. Mangu is basically mashed green plantains topped with vinegary onions, scrambled eggs, and chorizo. In this recipe, I use grapeseed oil and remove the sausage to make it leaner. And although it's typically served as a breakfast dish, it's wonderful for lunch or as a late-night snack, too.

SERVES: 4
TIME: 35 MINUTES

4 green unripe plantains
kosher salt
7 tablespoons grapeseed oil
2 large onions, cut in half and
  thinly sliced
1 tablespoon white vinegar
4 large eggs
thinly sliced scallions

Peel the plantains (see Tip, page 32) and cut them in half. Place the plantains in a pot, cover with water, and season with 2 tablespoons salt. Bring the water to a boil. When the plantains are tender, after about 10 minutes, drain the water and set the plantains aside in a large bowl.

Meanwhile, in a medium sauté pan, heat 2 tablespoons of the oil over medium-high heat. Add the onions and vinegar and season with salt. Cook for 5 to 7 minutes until softened, then set aside on a small plate.

In the same pan, heat 1 tablespoon of the oil over medium-high heat. Crack the eggs into a small bowl and beat. Pour the eggs into the hot pan and gently stir the egg mixture to form large, soft curds. Continue stirring until no visible liquid eggs remain, about 5 minutes total.

Mash the plantains with a fork or a potato masher. Add the remaining 4 tablespoons oil and 1 cup cold water and keep mashing until the consistency is very smooth. Serve the mashed plantains with the onions and eggs on top. Garnish with scallions.

"When I was first talking to my friends about this book, they all said, 'You can't make healthy mangu!' But really, what's so bad about it? Make the portions reasonable, and if you don't like all the egg yolks, just use two whole eggs and two whites. You'll still have the taste of scrambled eggs, but without all the cholesterol and fat."

Angie

BLACK BEANS & RICE

Angie

My grandmother Livia makes amazing black beans. But making beans with her was always such a process. She'd whip out the bag of beans from the pantry and scatter them onto a tray so we could pick out the rocks. Then she'd put them in a pot and we'd sit around the kitchen waiting for the beans to finish cooking. To this day, I don't know anyone whose black beans are more flavorful, soft, and creamy. Angelo's come a close second though and they're a whole lot easier to make!

SERVES: 6 TO 8
TIME: 1 HOUR 5 MINUTES

3 tablespoons olive oil
½ cup chopped onion
2 teaspoons chopped garlic
2 cups dried black beans, soaked overnight, rinsed and drained (see Tip)
4 sprigs fresh thyme
3 fresh or dried bay leaves
3 tablespoons distilled white vinegar
4½ cups chicken or vegetable stock
kosher salt
2 cups dry brown rice

Heat the olive oil in a medium pot over medium heat. When hot, add the onion and garlic and cook until softened, 3 to 5 minutes. Add the soaked beans, thyme, and 2 bay leaves and cook for 3 minutes. Stir in the vinegar and stock and simmer on low heat until the beans are soft and very tender, 90 minutes. Season with salt. The mixture should be soupy and the beans should still hold their shape.

Meanwhile, in a large pot, combine the brown rice and remaining bay leaf. Add 4 cups water to cover. Bring to a boil, then cover and simmer on low heat for 25 minutes or until tender. Remove from the heat and strain in a colander, if necessary. Set aside.

Serve the beans as a side or on top of brown rice or quinoa.

Tip HOW TO SOAK BEANS *Dried beans are an excellent source of fiber and protein. And because they're cheap and don't spoil, it's worth keeping a few bags of different varieties of dried beans in the pantry. To prepare, pick through the beans and remove any small stones. Place the beans in a large bowl and add enough water to cover by 1 inch. Soak the beans overnight. Drain the soaking water and start with fresh water to cook the beans. (For a quick soak, fill a large pot with beans and enough water to cover by 2 to 3 inches. Bring to a boil. Cook for 2 minutes. Remove from the heat and let stand for 1 hour. Drain the soaking water.)*

RED BEANS & RICE

Angie

Red beans and rice is another favorite comfort food. I love it because it's nostalgic, delicious, and really warms the soul. Typically rice and beans are made with fatty hunks of pork that swirl around the stew and admittedly impart a lot of flavor. But here my friend Margarita hooks up a version without the pork that still holds on to the traditional flavors that we all love so much. As she says, "Due to my daughter Maya's food allergies, I was quickly introduced to clean eating and all-natural food preparation. She really enjoys this version of rice and beans and I still get to pass on my Colombian heritage."

SERVES: 4 TO 8
TIME: 2 HOURS 20 MINUTES

2 tablespoons olive oil
1 large onion, finely chopped
1 green bell pepper, finely chopped
3 cloves garlic, minced
1 tablespoon ground cumin
1 tablespoon ground coriander
1 (8-ounce) can tomato sauce
1 cup dried red beans, soaked overnight (see Tip, page 117)
2 fresh or dried bay leaves
1 small bunch fresh thyme
1 teaspoon apple cider vinegar
kosher salt and freshly ground black pepper
cooked brown rice, to serve

In a medium heavy-bottomed pot, heat the olive oil over medium-high heat. Add the onion and bell pepper and cook until they become slightly soft and the onions become translucent, 5 to 7 minutes.

Add the garlic and cook for about 30 seconds, or until the garlic becomes fragrant. Stir in the cumin and coriander to coat the vegetables. Add the tomato sauce and stir again. Add the beans, 5 cups water, the bay leaves and thyme and give one last good stir.

Bring the mixture to a boil, then turn the heat to low. Cover and simmer until the beans are tender, about 2 hours. Add the vinegar and season with salt and pepper.

Serve with brown rice.

PIGEON PEA STEW

Angelo

Gandules, or pigeon peas, are a common ingredient in Latin American cooking. You'll often see them paired with rice in dishes like *arroz con gandules* or *moro de gandules*, a dish my family ate every Sunday. The peas are satisfying, supplying protein and color. If you can't find them fresh, look for canned varieties in Latin American markets. If using canned or precooked peas in this recipe, reduce the cooking time by half.

SERVES: 4
TIME: 1 HOUR 10 MINUTES

¼ cup chopped turkey bacon
2 tablespoons olive oil
3 cloves garlic, minced
1 medium onion, chopped
4 cups fresh green pigeon peas
½ teaspoon dried oregano
½ cup chopped fresh tomatoes
1 Thai chile pepper, chopped
3 tablespoons distilled white
   vinegar
4 sprigs fresh cilantro
kosher salt
cooked barley or brown rice,
   to serve

In a medium pot over medium heat, cook the turkey bacon to render out all the fat. Remove the bacon and set aside.

To the same pot, add the olive oil to the bacon grease, then add the garlic and onion. Cook over medium heat until slightly softened, about 3 minutes. Stir in the peas and oregano and cook for 1 to 2 minutes. Add the tomatoes, chile, vinegar, cilantro sprigs, and 6 cups water. Bring to a boil, then lower the heat and simmer, covered, for 30 minutes.

Return the bacon to the pot and cook until the peas are tender, about 15 minutes more. Season with salt. Serve with barley or brown rice.

KIDNEY BEAN SANCOCHO

Angelo

Sancocho is a stew that's cherished by Dominicans and served for special occasions. It's a stick-to-your-ribs kind of dish, made from many types of meat. You can think of it as the ultimate Dominican comfort food. To highlight the satisfying effect of beans and to offer a lighter, meatless alternative, I replaced the meat with red kidney beans. And to really make this dish unique, I added aromatic bitters to enhance the natural flavor of the beans. It can be served with a side of cooked brown rice or even tofu.

SERVES: 4 TO 6
TIME: 1 HOUR 40 MINUTES

¼ cup olive oil
2 tablespoons chopped garlic
1 tablespoon chopped fresh ginger
1 unripe green plantain, peeled and roughly chopped (see Tip, page 32)
½ pound yucca, peeled and roughly chopped
½ pound sweet potato, peeled and roughly chopped
1 medium green bell pepper, seeded and chopped
1 medium tomato, chopped
½ pound dried red kidney beans, soaked overnight (see Tip, page 117)
4 sprigs fresh flat-leaf parsley
2 sprigs fresh oregano
1 fresh or dried bay leaf
4 sprigs fresh cilantro, plus extra leaves for garnish
2 tablespoons aromatic bitters, optional (see right)
1 tablespoon sugar
kosher salt

Heat the olive oil in a large pot over medium-high heat. When hot, add the garlic and ginger and cook until just fragrant, 2 to 3 minutes. Stir in the plantain, yucca, sweet potato, bell pepper, tomato, and beans, and cook for another 5 minutes.

Add the parsley, oregano, bay leaf, cilantro, bitters, if using, and sugar along with 3 cups water and bring to a boil. Lower the heat and simmer until the beans are tender, 1 to 1½ hours. Season with salt.

To serve, garnish with fresh cilantro leaves.

WHAT ARE AROMATIC BITTERS?

Commonly found behind a bar, bitters are made from alcohol and plant extracts and are used in cocktails to enhance and round out flavors. They can be warm, spicy, and astringent, depending on the manufacturer. Find them at grocery stores in the beverage section or at liquor stores.

LATIN LETTUCE WRAPS
WITH LENTILS & AVOCADO

— *Angie*

I love these bean wraps because they're super filling and pack plenty of protein and fiber. They also don't leave me feeling uncomfortably full after lunch when I'm on-air for four hours and they'll get me through my shift without feeling hungry. You can make the lentils the night before to save time.

SERVES: 4
TIME: 40 MINUTES

1 cup dry lentils
½ teaspoon ground cumin, toasted
1 teaspoon kosher salt
1 tablespoon fresh lime juice
8 red-leaf lettuce leaves
1 cup alfalfa sprouts
8 sprigs fresh mint leaves
8 sprigs fresh cilantro leaves
1 ripe avocado, pitted and cut into 8 slices

Wash and drain the lentils. Pick over and remove any shriveled lentils, stones, and debris. Transfer to a medium saucepan and cover with 2 cups water. Bring to a boil, then reduce the heat and allow the lentils to simmer, uncovered, until tender, 20 to 30 minutes, adding more water if it becomes too dry. Let cool to room temperature.

In a small bowl, combine the cumin, salt, and lime juice.

Clean the lettuce leaves and pat dry. Holding a leaf in the palm of your hand, place ⅓ to ½ cup lentils in the leaf. Top with alfalfa sprouts, mint, cilantro, and avocado. Drizzle the lime dressing over the top. Repeat with the remaining leaves.

OVEN-ROASTED CHILES RELLENOS

— *Angelo*

Battered and fried, *chiles rellenos* are the ultimate Mexican comfort food. This lighter version is baked, allowing the flavors of the chile peppers, cheese, tomatoes, and garlic to shine through. Be sure to lightly roast the poblanos, which imparts a little smokiness to the dish.

SERVES: 2 TO 4
TIME: 55 MINUTES

4 medium poblano peppers
1 cup Oaxaca cheese (see page 27)
1 cup shredded Monterey Jack cheese
1 cup chopped tomatoes
1 tablespoon finely chopped garlic
1 teaspoon kosher salt

Preheat the oven to 350°F. Line a sheet tray with parchment paper or foil. Wipe the poblanos clean. Using tongs to hold one pepper at a time, roast over an open flame for 4 to 6 minutes to get a light char on the exterior.

Using a sharp knife, remove the top of the peppers, seeds, and membranes. Set aside.

In a small bowl, combine the cheeses, tomatoes, and garlic. Season the peppers with the salt, then stuff with the cheese-tomato mixture.

Bake until the peppers are tender and the cheese is bubbly, 30 to 45 minutes, depending on the size of the peppers.

We both love guacamole and dips so much that we thought they deserved their own section. In this chapter, we've created four exciting versions of guac that can be served individually or as a group with baked tortilla chips and veggies for dipping. But if avocados aren't your thing, we've also included several other delectable sauces, including three variations on mole, and salsas that can be used for dipping or for flavoring dishes and vinaigrettes. These recipes are so easy that you can get the kids involved. Make them together to create your own family food memories.

DIPS, CHIPS & SALSAS

Dips, Chips y Salsas

PINEAPPLE MARINADE

Angelo

The key to this marinade is the bromelain. You're probably scratching your head and thinking brom-a-whaa? It's an amazing enzyme found in pineapple that naturally tenderizes meat—and comes in handy in many recipes. Sometimes I'll save pineapple rind and add it to help braise tough meats. Beyond its tenderizing properties, pineapple lends a sweet and tart flavor to the meat. Its natural sugars also caramelize during the cooking process, giving proteins a nice charred quality. Try this pineapple marinade with skirt steak, chicken, fish, or even tofu. It's totally magical.

MAKES: 2¼ CUPS

TIME: 5 MINUTES

6 cloves garlic, coarsely
   chopped
½ cup minced yellow onion
1 cup pineapple puree
   (see Tip)
½ cup fresh lime juice
½ teaspoon ground cumin
1 teaspoon dried oregano
½ teaspoon lemon pepper
   seasoning
½ teaspoon freshly ground
   black pepper
1 teaspoon kosher salt
¼ cup chopped fresh cilantro
Tabasco sauce
½ cup olive oil

Pulse the garlic and onion in a blender until very finely chopped. Pour the pineapple puree and lime juice into the blender, then add the cumin, oregano, lemon pepper, black pepper, salt, and cilantro; season with Tabasco. Blend until thoroughly incorporated, scraping down the sides with a spatula. Add the olive oil and continue to blend until smooth. Transfer to an airtight container and refrigerate for up to 4 to 5 days.

Tip HOW TO MAKE PINEAPPLE PUREE *With a sharp knife, lop off the top of the pineapple and cut about a half inch off the bottom so it sits upright on a cutting board. Carefully cut the rind off in a downward motion, following the shape of the pineapple. Cut the pineapple into large chunks, discarding the core, and puree in a blender. Depending on how you plan to use the puree, you can strain it to make juice or leave it as is for a more rustic dish.*

GREEN SOFRITO

Angelo

Like *mirepoix* in French cuisine, *sofrito* serves as a foundation of flavor for braises, soups, and stews in Spanish, Portuguese, and Latin cuisines. The beauty of this sofrito is the use of fresh ingredients—jalapeños, tomatillos, and cilantro—that give it a vibrant green color and robust flavor. It also doesn't need to be cooked, making it an ideal sauce for finishing a dish. I like serving it with a beautiful piece of fish or meat.

MAKES: 2 CUPS
TIME: 10 MINUTES

1 medium white onion,
  cut in half
2 pounds tomatillos, husked,
  rinsed, and chopped
2 medium poblano peppers
2 medium jalapeños
6 cloves garlic
½ cup olive oil
¼ cup chopped fresh oregano
1 bunch fresh cilantro
  (stems and leaves)
2 tablespoons kosher salt
1 tablespoon ground
  white pepper

Preheat an outdoor grill or grill pan on medium-high heat. Place the onion halves cut-side down on the grill and cook until charred, about 5 minutes. Remove from the heat and place the grilled onion in a blender, along with the remaining ingredients. Blend until smooth.

Store the sofrito in the refrigerator for no longer than 2 days. Always serve chilled unless you're going to cook with it.

WHITE BEAN MOLE

Angelo

Mole is a chocolate-based sauce that's typically bitter and slightly spicy. It has a hint of underlying sweetness, but is generally used for savory dishes. In this version, I use starchy white beans to make the mole creamy. Beans also contribute dietary fiber and protein to this dish, making it healthy and satisfying. Use this as a dip or condiment for tacos, lettuce leaves, or plantain chips.

SERVES: 4 TO 6
TIME: 2 HOURS

2 medium dried ancho chile peppers
1 dried chipotle chile pepper
1 teaspoon cumin seeds, toasted and cooled
1 teaspoon dried oregano, crumbled
1 cinnamon stick, freshly grated
kosher salt
2 tablespoons olive oil
2 medium onions, chopped
4 cloves garlic, finely chopped
1 teaspoon grated orange zest
⅛ teaspoon sugar
3 tablespoons finely chopped unsweetened chocolate
1 (14½-ounce) can whole tomatoes in juice, chopped (reserve the juice)
1½ cups Great Northern beans, soaked overnight (see page 117)

Wipe all the dried chiles with a dry paper towel before using to remove any sandy particles on the surface. Make a lengthwise cut through each chile pepper and remove the stem and seeds.

Heat a medium-sized heavy skillet over medium heat. When hot, add the chiles. Using tongs, open them up and press them flat against the pan. Toast until the chiles are pliable and change slightly in color, about 30 seconds. Transfer to a plate and set aside to cool.

Tear the chiles into small pieces and place in a spice grinder. Add the cumin seeds and grind until the mixture is fine. Transfer to a small bowl and stir in the oregano, cinnamon stick, and 1½ teaspoons salt.

In a large heavy pot, heat the oil over medium-high heat. When hot, cook the onions until softened, 5 to 7 minutes, stirring occasionally. Add the garlic and cook for 1 minute. Season with the chile and spice blend and cook for another 30 seconds. Stir in the zest, sugar, chocolate, tomatoes with their juice, and 3 cups water and simmer, covered, for about 15 minutes, stirring occasionally. Stir in the beans and simmer on low heat until the beans are very soft and tender, 90 minutes. If the beans begin to look dry, add up to 1 cup water.

Puree the mixture in a food processor or blender. Season with salt. Serve warm, or transfer to an airtight container and refrigerate for up to 2 weeks.

CHARRED TOMATO MOLE

Angelo

Tomatoes have a lot of natural umami, a savory, meaty flavor that makes them so succulent and delicious. In the summer, when there's a bounty of fresh and delicious tomatoes, I like to make this sauce with dried ancho and guajillo chiles. It's so wonderfully fragrant and rich in flavor. Serve it with chicken, fish, or crispy tortillas.

SERVES: 4
TIME: 1 HOUR

5 dried ancho chile peppers
5 dried guajillo chile peppers
2 tablespoons slivered
  blanched almonds
2 tablespoons sesame seeds
1 pound plum tomatoes, cut in
  half lengthwise
½ pound tomatillos, husked,
  rinsed, and cut in half
¼ cup grapeseed oil
1 large onion, roughly chopped
8 cloves garlic, smashed
½ cup raisins
6 whole cloves
1 cinnamon stick
3 whole allspice berries
1 teaspoon dried oregano
1 tablespoon kosher salt
½ cup packed light brown
  sugar

Wipe all the dried chiles with a dry paper towel and cut off the tops with kitchen scissors. In a medium sauté pan over low heat, slowly toast the ancho and guajillo chiles, almonds, and sesame seeds until aromatic, 5 to 7 minutes. Transfer to a plate and set aside to cool.

Preheat a grill pan over medium-high heat. Add the tomatoes and tomatillos cut-side down and char on all sides until the exterior is black. Decrease the heat to medium and add the oil and onion to the pan. Slowly cook until the onion is softened, about 5 minutes. Turn the heat to low and add the remaining ingredients. Stir to combine and cook for 25 minutes.

Remove the tomato mixture from the heat and discard the cinnamon stick. Puree in a food processor until smooth, about 1 minute. Serve warm or cold. Keep in an airtight container in the refrigerator for up to 2 weeks.

Nutritional Note ✳

Tomatoes are rich in lycopene, an antioxidant compound that gives them their rich, red color. In some studies, lycopene has been shown to help fight certain cancers. To maximize your absorption of lycopene, eat cooked tomatoes. Cooking breaks down the cell walls that trap lycopene, making it more available to your body.

CARROT MOLE
WITH TOASTED PUMPKIN SEED VINAIGRETTE

Angelo

Carrots are an indispensible part of every kitchen. Not only are they used to flavor stocks, stews, and roasts, they also serve as nutritious snacks for kids and adults alike. For this dish, I wanted to bring carrots to the forefront. They have an earthiness about them and an intriguing sweet flavor that's so undervalued. Once cooked and pureed, the crisp carrot is transformed into a bright and smooth puree that complements the crunchy pumpkin seed vinaigrette in this dish.

SERVES: 2 TO 4
TIME: 40 MINUTES

PEPITA VINAIGRETTE

3 tablespoons raw green
   pumpkin seeds (pepitas)
¼ cup balsamic vinegar
3 tablespoons sugar
¼ teaspoon kosher salt
1 teaspoon chopped fresh
   thyme leaves

CARROT MOLE

3 tablespoons olive oil
2 tablespoons chopped onion
1 teaspoon chopped garlic
1 teaspoon chopped fresh
   ginger
½ cinnamon stick
½ fresh nutmeg, grated
½ teaspoon ground coriander
½ teaspoon chipotle chile
   powder
1 teaspoon sesame seeds
2 cups grated carrots
1 cup vegetable or chicken
   stock
3 tablespoons sugar
kosher salt

In a small pan over low heat, lightly toast the pumpkin seeds for 2 to 3 minutes. Remove from the heat and place in a bowl with the remaining vinaigrette ingredients. Stir together and set aside.

In a medium pot, heat the oil over medium-high heat. When hot, add the onion, garlic, ginger, cinnamon stick, nutmeg, coriander, chipotle powder, and sesame seeds. Cook until the onions are tender and the spices are aromatic, 5 to 7 minutes. Lower the heat to medium, add the carrots and cook for another 5 minutes. Add the stock and sugar, and cook until the carrots are completely tender, about 10 minutes more. Place in a blender and puree until smooth. Season with salt.

Transfer the mole to a serving bowl and drizzle the vinaigrette on top. Serve with grilled steak, lettuce leaves, tostones (page 32), or whole-wheat tortilla chips (page 132).

RUSTIC WHOLE-WHEAT TORTILLA CHIPS

It's easy enough to break into a bag of tortilla chips, but they're often loaded with unnecessary fat and sodium. So, rather than give up chips, I came up with this super-easy recipe using whole-wheat tortillas. Just place the whole tortillas in the oven and bake. You don't need to brush or spray any oil on them—they'll crisp up and become crunchy. And, unlike store-bought chips, which are flaky and thin, these have substance. Serve with guacamole (pages 135 to 138) or salsa (page 141). This is super easy to get kids involved, as my friend Margarita did with her daughter, Maya, at right.

SERVES: 2 TO 4
TIME: 15 MINUTES

Two (8-inch) whole-wheat tortillas

Preheat the oven to 350°F.

Place the tortillas directly on the oven rack. Bake until they are dry and crispy, about 15 minutes. Break into pieces and serve warm with guacamole or salsa. Store in an airtight container for up to 3 days.

Nutritional Note ✱ Whole-wheat tortillas are packed with more fiber and nutrients than plain flour tortillas. Use them for roll-up sandwiches, burritos, tacos, and chips.

GUACAMOLE TRADITIONAL

Angie

Do not ever buy store-bought guac! Whip up this super-easy version instead—it's healthy, tasty, and everyone loves it. Serve it with my Rustic Whole-Wheat Tortilla Chips (page 132) and you will be treated like a rock star.

SERVES: 4
TIME: 10 MINUTES

2 ripe avocados
3 tablespoons minced
   jalapeño
¼ cup fresh lime juice
3 tablespoons minced red
   onion
3 tablespoons chopped
   cilantro
1 teaspoon kosher salt,
   or more to taste

With a sharp knife, cut the avocados in half lengthwise. Remove the pit and, with a spoon, scrape the flesh into a small bowl. Transfer half to a medium bowl and use the back of a fork to mash it until a paste forms. Add the jalapeño, lime juice, onion, cilantro, and salt and stir to combine.

Add the reserved avocado half, mix gently, and season with salt, as needed.

Tip ADDING COLOR *For great color and unexpected sweetness, toss some pomegranate seeds into the guacamole.*

GUACAMOLE VERDE
WITH TOMATILLO

Angelo

It's pretty hard to get a perfectly ripe avocado at the grocery store. But a trick I learned for speeding up the ripening process is to put them in paper bags with apples or bananas. Those fruits release ethylene gas, which can help soften rock-hard avocados

SERVES: 4
TIME: 5 MINUTES

3 ripe avocados
2 tablespoons diced red onion
3 tablespoons fresh lime juice
3 tablespoons finely chopped
   fresh cilantro
¼ cup diced tomatillo
½ teaspoon kosher salt,
   or more to taste
3 tablespoons Cotija cheese
   (see page 27)

With a sharp knife, cut the avocados in half lengthwise. Remove the pit and, with a spoon, scrape the flesh into a small bowl. Transfer half to a medium bowl and use the back of a fork to mash it until a paste forms. Add the onion, lime juice, cilantro, tomatillo, and salt and stir to combine. Add the reserved avocado half, mix gently, and season with more salt, if needed.

Transfer the guacamole to a serving bowl and garnish with the cheese.

GUACAMOLE VERDE
WITH TOASTED PUMPKIN SEEDS & CHEESE

— *Angelo*

The addition of pumpkin seeds and Manchego cheese to this guacamole was inspired by a dish that I had in Baja, Mexico. Pepitas, or pumpkin seeds, are widely popular in Mexican cuisine and can be eaten alone or tossed into salads and mole sauce. Not only do they contain healthy fats, they also pack in protein, iron, fiber, and zinc to keep us in great shape. I like to serve this with chips or lettuce leaves.

SERVES: 4
TIME: 10 MINUTES

3 ripe avocados
2 tablespoons chopped
    red onion
2 tablespoons fresh lime juice
1 teaspoon kosher salt,
    or more to taste
3 tablespoons chopped
    tomatillo
1 tablespoon chopped fresh
    cilantro
2 tablespoons toasted hulled
    pumpkin seeds (pepitas)
2 tablespoons grated
    Manchego cheese

Cut the avocados in half lengthwise. Remove the pit and, with a spoon, scrape the flesh into a small bowl. Transfer half to a medium bowl and use the back of a fork to mash it until a paste forms.

Add the onion, lime juice, and salt and mix. Add the reserved avocado half, mix gently, and season with more salt, if needed.

Transfer the guacamole to a serving bowl and garnish with the remaining ingredients.

"One of the great things I've learned from Angelo is to not be afraid to add different textures and flavors to guacamole. At his restaurant Añejo, he makes one with pomegranate seeds sprinkled on top that I rave about all the time. This guacamole is another one of my favorites. The toasted pumpkin seeds and manchego cheese are not typical, but they are a tasty surprise."

— *Angie*

GUACAMOLE
WITH A TRIO OF CHILES

Angie

Not sure if your avocados are ripe enough? Here's what I do to check: If the avocado feels like your forehead, it's not ready; if it feels like your cheek, it's too old; if it feels like your nose, it's just right. You got that? I like to eat this guac with steamed tortillas or wrapped in lettuce.

SERVES: 4 TO 6
TIME: 5 MINUTES

4 ripe avocados
3 tablespoons diced red onion
1 tablespoon diced serrano chile pepper
1 tablespoon diced jalapeño
1 tablespoon chopped fresh cilantro
2 tablespoons diced tomato
1 teaspoon kosher salt, or more to taste
1 teaspoon finely chopped chipotle in adobo

With a sharp knife, cut the avocados in half lengthwise. Remove the pit and, with a spoon, scrape the flesh into a small bowl. Transfer half to a medium bowl and use the back of a fork to mash it until a paste forms. Add the rest of the ingredients and stir to combine.

Add the reserved avocado half, mix gently, and season with more salt, if needed.

CAPER & OLIVE VERDE SAUCE

Angelo

I was inspired to make this smoky, chunky, briny sauce by a trip that I took to Veracruz, Mexico. It includes capers, one of my favorite ingredients. I like brined capers, as opposed to salt-packed ones, because you can save the brining liquid for dressings or vinaigrettes. Serve this with fresh vegetables, grilled fish, chicken, or beef, or even with a good whole-wheat baguette.

MAKES: ½ CUP
TIME: 20 MINUTES

1 poblano pepper
½ cup capers, rinsed
¼ cup pitted green olives
¼ cup chopped fresh cilantro
1 medium jalapeño, finely chopped
2 sprigs fresh thyme, leaves removed and finely chopped
3 tablespoons fresh lime juice
¼ cup olive oil
¼ teaspoon kosher salt

Turn a gas burner on medium-high heat. Holding the poblano with tongs, place it directly over the burner. Roast until the skin is blackened, 8 to 10 minutes, turning occasionally. Let cool slightly, then remove the stem and seeds and roughly chop.

In a large mortar, combine the poblano with the remaining ingredients. Mash with the pestle. (You can also use a food processor.) Mix well and chill for up to 2 days.

WATERMELON & CHIPOTLE SALSA

— *Angelo*

SERVES: 4
TIME: 15 MINUTES

2 cups diced watermelon
1 tablespoon chipotle chile powder (see below)
3 tablespoons extra-virgin olive oil
1 large vine-ripened tomato, cored and coarsely chopped
¼ medium red onion, thinly sliced
¼ medium jalapeño, thinly sliced
1 teaspoon chopped fresh oregano
½ teaspoon kosher salt
2 tablespoons lime juice

It might sound strange, but pairing sweet and juicy watermelon with smoky chipotle really works! To make this truly exceptional, let the chipotle and watermelon sit together for at least 10 minutes, which allows the heat and smokiness of the chile to really sink into the flesh of the melon. This is great with grilled fish, but you could also just add raw fish to make a ceviche.

Place the watermelon in a medium bowl, add the chipotle powder and olive oil, and stir gently to combine. Marinate for 10 minutes.

Fold in the tomato, onion, jalapeño, oregano, and salt. Add the lime juice just before serving.

WHAT IS A CHIPOTLE?

Chipotle peppers are red jalapeños that have been slowly smoked and roasted, resulting in a smoky, distinctly flavored dried pepper that packs mild heat. Chipotles are often used in Mexican and Tex-Mex cooking for salsas, marinades, and stews. They're found whole, ground, or canned with adobo sauce at most supermarkets (in the international section), Latin markets, or online.

CHARRED TOMATO & GREEN OLIVE SALSA

— *Angelo*

SERVES: 6 TO 8
TIME: 15 MINUTES

1 pound plum tomatoes, sliced in half lengthwise
1 onion, cut in half
4 cloves garlic, peeled
1 teaspoon toasted cumin seeds
¼ cup green pitted olives
1 teaspoon chopped fresh thyme
1 tablespoon chopped fresh cilantro
2 tablespoons olive oil
kosher salt

Grilling the tomatoes, onions, and garlic softens the textures and gives this condiment a nice smoky flavor without any added fat. It also mellows out the raw flavors, bringing out the sweetness. Serve with a beautiful piece of grilled fish or simply with chips.

Preheat an outdoor grill or a sauté pan to high heat. Place the tomatoes and onion cut-side down on the grill or pan and cook until charred, 5 to 8 minutes. Remove from the heat and then char the garlic cloves.

Transfer the charred tomatoes, onion, and garlic to a blender and add the remaining ingredients. Pulse a few times for a chunky consistency. Season with salt and pulse again to combine.

No meal is complete without dessert, but Latin sweets can be overly sugary and heavy. Our solution was to use healthier ingredients to create these light and modern takes on some of our favorite classics. For many of our treats, we take advantage of the sweetness and tropical flavor of fruits commonly found in the Latin American diet. Try them all and discover guilt-free, healthy ways to finish a meal.

DESSERTS

Postre

SLOW-ROASTED PLANTAINS
WITH AGAVE PINEAPPLE SAUCE

— *Angie*

Plantanos, or plantains, are a nutritious staple in all Latin American cuisines. You can use them at any stage of ripeness (just don't eat them raw!) to make a snack, side, or main. I'd never thought to use plantains in a dessert until Angelo suggested it, but why not? For this recipe, you'll want to use really ripe plantains—the skins will look black—that are naturally sweet so you don't need to use too much added sugar.

SERVES: 2
TIME: 30 MINUTES

2 ripe plantains
½ cup agave nectar
1 tablespoon kosher salt
¼ cup pineapple puree
   (see Tip, page 126)

Preheat the oven to 350°F.

With a fork, lightly pierce the skin on all sides of the plantains. Place them on a rimmed baking sheet and roast for about 25 minutes, turning occasionally.

Meanwhile, in a small saucepan over medium heat, bring the agave, salt, and pineapple puree to a simmer. Remove from the heat.

As the plantains are roasting, glaze each with the agave mixture. (It's important that the plantain skins are pierced so that the agave mixture can sweeten the fruit inside.) The plantains are done when the flesh is fork tender and the skin is shiny and turns a deep charcoal color.

Place the hot and blackened plantains on a plate and split the skins open. Serve with additional warm pineapple sauce on the side.

MY FAVORITE FLAN

Angelo

The silky-smooth texture is my favorite part of this dessert. To get it right, you need to bake the flan in a water bath, a slow and gentle way of cooking that tones down the aggressiveness of the heat so the eggs don't curdle. This lighter version of traditional flan includes reduced-fat cream cheese to add creaminess and body, as well as tanginess. This dessert might taste a bit lighter, but it is every bit as flavorful and voluptuous as the original.

SERVES: 10
TIME: 1 HOUR 15 MINUTES, PLUS CHILLING

nonstick cooking spray
1 cup sugar
8 ounces reduced-fat cream cheese, at room temperature
6 large eggs
1 (14-ounce) can nonfat or low-fat sweetened condensed milk
1 (12-ounce) can nonfat or low-fat evaporated milk
2 teaspoons pure vanilla extract
¼ cup grated Cotija cheese (see page 27)

Preheat the oven to 350°F. Coat 10 (6-ounce) ramekins or baking cups with nonstick cooking spray and set in a large roasting pan.

In a small heavy-bottomed saucepan over medium heat, combine the sugar and ¼ cup water and gently swirl the pan so that the sugar dissolves. While continuously swirling the pan, cook the sugar until it turns amber in color, 10 to 12 minutes. Carefully pour enough caramel into the ramekins to coat the bottom of each.

In a large bowl, with an electric mixer at medium-high speed, beat the cream cheese until soft and smooth. Beat in the eggs, one at a time, until thoroughly combined, scraping down the sides with a spatula. Add the condensed milk, evaporated milk, and vanilla extract; mix to combine.

Pour about ½ cup custard into each of the prepared ramekins. Fill the roasting pan with enough hot water so that it comes 1 inch up the sides of the ramekins. Bake until a knife inserted into the middle of the flan comes out clean, about 45 minutes.

Carefully remove the ramekins from the water bath and cool on a wire rack. When cool, cover and refrigerate for at least 3 hours.

To serve, run a knife around each flan and invert onto a serving plate, allowing the caramel to run down the sides. Scatter cheese on top.

"Flan is one of my favorite desserts, and I love the light, yet creamy texture of this version. It's like a cross between a traditional flan and a cheesecake. The addition of Cotija cheese threw me off a little at first, but I love the way sweet and salty work together in this dessert."

Angie

SILKEN SOY & ALMOND MILK FLAN

Angie

Many Latinos suffer from lactose intolerance, a condition that makes dairy products hard to digest. So, as an alternative, we've substituted soy and almond milks in this tasty dessert. I was skeptical about the results at first, but you literally can't taste the difference at all. Feel free to use just soy or almond milk if you prefer one over the other.

SERVES: 6
TIME: 1 HOUR 30 MINUTES

nonstick cooking spray
1 cup sugar
½ vanilla bean
1 cup unsweetened low-fat
    soy milk
1 cup unsweetened
    almond milk
⅛ teaspoon ground cinnamon
⅛ teaspoon freshly grated
    nutmeg
⅛ teaspoon fine salt
2 large eggs
2 large egg yolks

Preheat the oven to 300°F. Coat 6 (6-ounce) ramekins with nonstick cooking spray and set in a large roasting pan.

In a small heavy-bottomed saucepan over medium heat, combine ¼ cup of the sugar and ¼ cup water and gently swirl the pan so that the sugar dissolves. While continuously swirling the pan, cook the sugar until it turns amber in color, 10 to 12 minutes. Carefully pour enough caramel into the ramekins to coat the bottom of each.

Run the tip of a sharp knife down the length of the half vanilla bean. Split the vanilla bean in half lengthwise and scrape out the seeds.

In a medium pot over medium heat, warm the soy and almond milks, remaining ¾ cup sugar, vanilla bean and seeds, cinnamon, nutmeg, and salt for 5 to 8 minutes, stirring to dissolve the sugar. In a medium heatproof bowl, whisk the egg and egg yolks. Pour about 1 cup of the hot milk mixture over the yolks and whisk vigorously to combine. When the eggs are tempered, add the remainder of the milk mixture. Strain to remove the half vanilla bean pod and divide the milk mixture evenly among the ramekins in the roasting pan.

Pour boiling water into the roasting pan to come halfway up the sides of the ramekins. Bake until the flan is almost set, 50 to 60 minutes. Carefully remove the ramekins from the water bath and cool on a wire rack. When cool, cover and refrigerate for at least 3 hours.

To serve, run a knife around each flan and invert onto a serving plate, allowing the caramel to run down the sides.

COCONUT & BARLEY PUDDING

Angelo

This beautiful dish was inspired by *tembleque*, a coconut dessert from Puerto Rico. I gave it a nutritious twist by adding whole-grain barley and sweet corn. Besides adding fiber, nutrients, and wonderful flavor, these two additions give a chewy and crunchy texture, making it also fun to eat!

SERVES: 4
TIME: 15 MINUTES

½ teaspoon cornstarch
1 cup light coconut milk
¼ cup cooked hulled barley
⅓ cup sugar
¼ cup fresh or frozen sweet
  corn kernels
¼ cup unsweetened coconut
  flakes

In a small bowl, combine 3 tablespoons water and the cornstarch. Stir until the cornstarch is dissolved.

In a medium saucepan over low heat, combine the coconut milk, ¾ cup water, the barley, and sugar. Stir with a heatproof spatula until the sugar is dissolved, and then bring to a boil. Add the corn kernels and cornstarch mixture, stirring it in quickly to avoid lumps. Return the mixture to a boil, then simmer until thickened, stirring constantly, about 2 minutes. Pour the pudding into ramekins or a serving bowl and set aside at room temperature.

In a medium sauté pan over medium heat, lightly toast the coconut flakes; they should be lightly browned and have a nutty aroma. Let cool.

Sprinkle the top of each pudding with the toasted coconut and serve.

SWEET LENTIL & CLOVE PUDDING

Angelo

Packed with satisfying protein and fiber, beans are typically used in savory dishes. But in Asian cooking, they're used a lot for desserts. This is a riff on a Chinese bean soup that uses green mung or red beans. In this version, I use lentils and red kidney beans to create texture and visual interest, and flavor it with cloves, cinnamon, and allspice to give it a Latin twist.

SERVES: 2
TIME: 1 HOUR 45 MINUTES

2 cups dried lentils
½ cup dried red kidney beans,
  soaked overnight (see Tip,
  page 117)
4 cups low-fat (1%) milk
¼ cup sugar
¼ cup agave nectar
⅛ teaspoon salt
4 whole cloves
1 stick cinnamon
4 allspice berries

Combine all the ingredients in a medium pot and bring to a boil. Lower the heat and simmer until the beans are tender, 60 to 90 minutes; the mixture should resemble a thick soup. Remove from the heat and let cool to room temperature.

To serve, discard the spices and ladle the pudding into small bowls.

SPICY MANGO PUDDING

Angelo

In the Dominican Republic, mangoes grew near my paternal aunt and uncle's house in the mountains. The fruits were so plump and ripe that the second you cut into one, the juice would be all over you. I took walks just to pull them off the trees for a quick snack. Inspired by this memory, I came up with this light dessert that highlights the sweetness of the fruit, along with the nuttiness of the coconut milk and heat of the chile.

SERVES: 4
TIME: 45 MINUTES

2 ripe mangoes, peeled and
   seeded (see Tip)
1 Thai chile pepper
1 tablespoon powdered gelatin
⅓ cup sugar
1 cup light coconut milk

In a blender, puree the mangoes and chile until smooth. Transfer the puree to a large bowl.

In a small saucepan over medium-high heat, bring ½ cup water to a rolling boil. Remove from the heat and whisk in the gelatin, mixing quickly to avoid lumps. Stir in the sugar until dissolved. Pour the mixture into the bowl with the pureed mango and stir well. Add the coconut milk and continue to stir until well combined.

Pour the pudding into glasses and chill in the refrigerator until set, 15 to 20 minutes.

Tip HOW TO PEEL AND SEED A MANGO *Depending on whether you're cooking or eating the mango, there are two ways to do this. The first way, which is preferred for this recipe, is to cut ¼ inch off the stem end to create a flat surface. With the mango standing upright, take a sharp knife and slice the peel off in a downward motion, following the shape of the mango. Once peeled, slice the flesh from around the seed.*

To peel a mango for eating, stand it upright (there's no need to create the flat bottom) and slice down one side of the pit. Repeat on the other side. You should end up with three pieces: the pit and two halves. Score the halves and spoon out the cubes of mango from the skins, then cut off the flesh from around the pit.

SPICY DARK CHOCOLATE TAMALES

Angelo

Sometimes called "the food of the gods," chocolate has been highly valued by Latin Americans for hundreds of years. The Aztecs and Mayas used cacao beans in religious ceremonies, and the Aztecs even used the beans as currency. Today, chocolate may not be quite so important to us, but I love its rich, complex flavor, and health benefits. This ridiculously delicious dessert uses antioxidant-rich dark chocolate, and to help cut down on saturated fat, I replace half the butter with canola oil, one of the healthiest oils.

MAKES: 18 TAMALES
TIME: 30 MINUTES, PLUS SOAKING AND CHILLING

20 corn husks
8 ounces dark chocolate (preferably more than 60% cocoa), chopped
4 ounces (1 stick) unsalted butter, at room temperature
½ cup canola oil
⅓ cup sugar
1½ teaspoons baking powder
1 teaspoon kosher salt
½ teaspoon chipotle chile powder
2 pounds prepared masa harina (see page 27)
¼ to ½ cup low-fat (1%) milk

In a medium bowl, cover the corn husks with hot water. Let soak for at least 30 minutes to soften.

Place half the chocolate in a medium saucepan over medium-low heat, then add the butter, oil, sugar, baking powder, salt, and chipotle powder. Whisk the ingredients together until the chocolate is melted and the mixture is smooth, 5 to 7 minutes. Remove from the heat and let cool.

Place the masa harina in a large bowl. Stir in the chocolate mixture until well incorporated. Fold in the remainder of the chocolate. Add ¼ cup of the milk, stirring, until the dough comes together. Add up to another ¼ cup for the dough to be sticky, but still hold its shape. Chill, covered, for 45 minutes.

When you're ready to assemble the tamales, tear two of the corn husks into 9 strips each. Equally divide the masa among the remaining corn husks, leaving a 1-inch border at the tapered end of each husk and around the sides. Place the chocolate mixture in the middle of the masa, equally dividing it among the tamales. Wrap each tamale by bringing in the two long sides and rolling the bundle up. Tie with a strip of corn husk.

Place the tamales in a steamer basket set over a pot of simmering water. Steam for 35 to 40 minutes. Check the water periodically and refill if necessary. The tamales are done when the husk can be easily peeled away. Let the tamales sit for 10 minutes before serving.

EXOTIC FRUIT SALAD
WITH BASIL-CILANTRO SUGAR

— *Angie*

SERVES: 4
TIME: 5 MINUTES

1 large pineapple, peeled and cut into ¼-inch-thick slices
4 passion fruit, cut in half
1 mango, peeled and cut into large chunks (see Tip, page 150)
4 lychee fruits, peeled
3 sprigs fresh basil leaves
5 sprigs fresh cilantro leaves
¼ cup sugar

If my son, Niko, had his way, he'd eat mac and cheese every day! But that doesn't mean it'll always be that way—kids change their minds about foods any second of any day, so that's why it's so important to keep introducing them to new ones. Let your kid pick what they want to eat but don't pressure them to eat it all. I tried this salad on Niko and, although he was initially skeptical, he ended up eating some of the mango. That's a win in my book!

Arrange the pineapple, passion fruit, mango, and lychees on a large platter.

Combine the basil, cilantro, and sugar in the bowl of a food processor. Pulse until completely blended, about 30 seconds. Sprinkle a tablespoon of the herb sugar over the fruit and serve.

GRILLED PINEAPPLE
WITH ANCHO AGAVE SYRUP

— *Angie*

You often hear about grilling vegetables and meat, but what about fruit? In this recipe, we grilled pineapple to bring out its natural sweetness and to impart a nice smoky flavor. Serve this for dessert or as an accompaniment to a main course or salad.

SERVES: 4 TO 6
TIME: 15 MINUTES

1 medium pineapple
¼ cup ancho chile peppers (about 4 chiles)
1 teaspoon ground cumin
½ cup agave nectar
½ teaspoon kosher salt

Preheat an outdoor grill or grill pan to medium-high heat.

Peel the pineapple and cut crosswise into ¼-inch-thick slices. Lay the slices on a sheet tray.

Wipe the dried chiles with a dry paper towel to remove any sandy particles on the surface. In a blender, pulse the chiles to create a fine chile powder. Add the cumin, agave, and salt and blend until smooth.

Lightly drizzle the syrup over the pineapple. Grill the pineapple for 3 minutes per side or until grill marks appear on the fruit. Transfer to a platter and drizzle a generous amount of syrup over the fruit.

TRES LECHES SHAKE

Angie

Inspired by the popular tres leches cake, we came up with this milkshake that uses three different milks: regular, coconut, and condensed. Although Greek yogurt is not really Latin, it provides a little tanginess to cut through the sweetness, along with satisfying protein. Make it a little boozy by adding a shot of rum or tequila reposado, an aged tequila that has a smooth taste.

SERVES: 1
TIME: 5 MINUTES

¼ cup nonfat Greek yogurt
1 cup low-fat (1%) milk
½ cup unsweetened coconut
  milk (from well-shaken can)
1 tablespoon nonfat
  sweetened condensed milk
½ ounce dark rum or tequila
  reposado, optional
ice cubes

Place all the ingredients in a blender. Blend until smooth. Pour into a tall glass and serve with a straw.

MEXICAN ICE
WITH GUAVA & PINEAPPLE

Angelo

Angie's not a big fan of spicy heat, but she loved the addition of chipotle in adobo for this dessert. It adds smokiness to the sweet and tropical flavors of the fruit, and the cooling sensation of the ice tames the heat of the chile pepper. Serve it as a refreshing treat on a hot summer day.

SERVES: 4
TIME: 30 MINUTES, PLUS FREEZING

3 cups pineapple puree
   (see Tip, page 126)
1 cup guava paste
   (see Tip, page 64)
1 teaspoon finely chopped
   chipotle in adobo
½ teaspoon kosher salt
¼ cup sugar
1 cinnamon stick

In a medium pot over medium heat, combine all of the ingredients. Once the mixture comes to a simmer, remove from the heat and cover. Let sit for 20 minutes.

Strain into a shallow container, discarding the cinnamon stick, and freeze for 4 to 6 hours. Once the mixture is frozen, use a fork to scrape the ice. Scoop into serving bowls.

LATINO MANGO CAKE

Angie

Mangoes are one of my favorite fruits, so I was thrilled to find a fruit stand near the station that sold the best mangoes. They were amazing—so juicy and ripe. I bought them all the time and, for a month straight, I literally had a mango a day! I even made the mistake of trying to drive while eating a mango—not my best decision but clearly I was obsessed. In this recipe, you won't have to worry about that because the mango is neatly tucked into the cake.

SERVES: 6
TIME: 50 MINUTES

nonstick cooking spray
½ cup plus 2 tablespoons
  all-purpose flour
¼ teaspoons baking powder
¼ teaspoon kosher salt
¼ teaspoon ground cinnamon
¼ teaspoon ground nutmeg
¼ cup sugar
¼ cup packed brown sugar
⅓ cup vegetable oil
1 large egg
1 cup chopped fresh mango
  (see Tip, page 150)
¼ cup chopped jalapeño,
  optional

CAKE ACCOMPANIMENTS

Serve this cake with a fruit compote made from fresh berries mashed with sugar and herbs; a dusting of confectioners' sugar; or—Angelo's first choice—fresh chopped mangoes tossed with a little sugar and chile powder.

Preheat the oven to 375°F. Grease a 6-inch round cake pan with nonstick cooking spray.

In a medium bowl, combine the flour, baking powder, salt, cinnamon, and nutmeg and mix well.

In another medium bowl, mix together the sugars, oil, and egg. Fold the dry ingredients into the wet until combined. Stir in the mango and jalapeño, if using, until just combined.

Pour the batter into the prepared pan and bake until a toothpick inserted into the center of the cake comes out clean, 25 to 30 minutes. Remove from the oven and cool in pan on a wire rack for 10 minutes. Run a thin knife around the cake to loosen it from the pan and invert. Cool completely on the wire rack.

When cool, place the cake onto a platter and see the suggestions for accompaniments at left.

We love cocktails, so it's no surprise that we had a lot of fun developing recipes for this chapter! These drinks are amazing—so light and refreshing and full of flavor, but without all the sugar and calories of so many other drinks out there. And because cocktails aren't for everyone, we also came up several nonalcoholic drinks that can be enjoyed by the whole family. Go ahead and make one (or two, or three) now!

DRINKS

Bebidas

BARLEY HORCHATA

Angelo

A great Mexican classic, traditionally *horchata* is a creamy, milk-based drink made with toasted rice. This version is healthier and more delectable because of the addition of barley, which adds a beautiful viscosity to the drink. Trust me, this will become a family favorite.

SERVES: 4
TIME: 15 MINUTES

1½ cups dried hulled barley
1 cinnamon stick, plus more
   for grating
2 whole allspice berries
4 cups low-fat (1%) milk
½ cup agave nectar

In a large sauté pan over medium heat, lightly toast the barley for 5 minutes, while continually shaking the pan. Add the cinnamon stick and allspice and toast for an additional 2 minutes, or until fragrant.

Add the milk and agave to the pan, reduce the heat to low, and simmer for 5 minutes. Discard the cinnamon stick and allspice before transferring to a blender. Blend until smooth and strain through a fine-mesh sieve.

To serve, garnish with freshly grated cinnamon. Drink chilled or warm.

LOW-FAT COQUITO

Angie

The holidays are a time to celebrate and enjoy the finer things in life—like eating—so who wants to count calories? At my family gatherings, I usually bring a bottle of *coquito*. Made from coconut, milk, cinnamon, and rum, it's a creamy Puerto Rican eggnog. Here's a guilt-free version that my family still thinks is the original (shhh!) and, honestly, I think it tastes better. Light and airy, it pairs perfectly with appetizers, mains, and desserts. So, serve it on the rocks and you're good to go!

MAKES: 11 (5-OUNCE) DRINKS
TIME: 5 MINUTES, PLUS CHILLING

1 (12-ounce) can fat-free
   evaporated milk
1 (14-ounce) can fat-free
   sweetened condensed milk
1 (14-ounce) can light coconut
   milk
½ cup pasteurized egg
   substitute
½ teaspoon ground cinnamon,
   plus more for garnish
1 teaspoon pure vanilla extract
1 cup dark rum
13 cinnamon sticks

In a blender, blend the evaporated milk, condensed milk, coconut milk, egg substitute, ground cinnamon, vanilla extract, and rum until light and frothy, about 3 minutes. Transfer to an airtight container and add 2 cinnamon sticks. Refrigerate for at least 2 hours.

To serve, pour the drink into individual glasses and garnish each with a cinnamon stick and a sprinkle of ground cinnamon.

Tip EXTRACTING FLAVOR *Leave the* coquito *in the fridge for up to 2 days before serving. The cinnamon sticks will continue to infuse additional flavor into the drink.*

Nutritional Note ✳ *My version of this drink cuts 270 calories from the original and almost 7 grams of fat.*

CHIPOTLE PASSION FRUIT MICHELADA

Angelo

If you're not familiar with the *michelada*, it's a beer-based Mexican cocktail made from lime juice, hot sauce, Worcestershire, and, of course, beer. Like Bloody Marys, you can make many riffs on the classic; here's mine. It includes passion fruit to provide tart and tangy notes to the drink, along with chipotle salt to give it some heat and smokiness.

SERVES: 2
TIME: 5 MINUTES

1 tablespoon chipotle chile powder
¼ cup kosher salt
2 wedges of lime, plus ¼ cup fresh lime juice
ice cubes
12 ounces Mexican beer
¼ cup passion fruit puree
2 teaspoons Worcestershire
2 teaspoons Tabasco sauce

In a wide, shallow dish, mix the chipotle powder and salt. Run a wedge of lime around the rim of a glass, then dip in the salt mixture. Carefully fill the glass with ice cubes and set aside. Repeat with a second glass.

In a pitcher, combine the lime juice, beer, passion fruit puree, Worcestershire and Tabasco sauces. Pour into the prepared glasses and serve.

TAMARIND SOUR PUNCH

Angelo

Some call it tamarindo, I call it tamarind. A large tree commonly found in the tropics, the tamarind yields an aromatic and sour tasting pulp that's fibrous and sticky. In this recipe, the sourness is balanced by the sweetness of the guava and the warming notes of the allspice, cinnamon, and cumin to make a refreshing summer drink. And of course, in Angie's home, you would add rum.

SERVES: 8 TO 10
TIME: 10 MINUTES

1 cup tamarind paste (see Tip)
½ cup guava paste (see Tip, page 64)
6 cups soda water
½ cup agave nectar
2 whole cloves
2 allspice berries
1 cinnamon stick
¼ teaspoon cumin seeds
½ cup light rum, optional
ice cubes
8 to 10 sprigs fresh mint

In a punch bowl or 2-quart pitcher, combine the tamarind and guava pastes, soda water, and agave and mix well.

In a small sauté pan over medium heat, lightly toast the cloves, allspice, cinnamon stick, and cumin seeds for 2 minutes, or until fragrant. Add the toasted spices and the rum, if using, to the punch bowl.

Serve the punch over ice and garnish each drink with a sprig of mint.

Tip BUYING TAMARIND PASTE *Look for large blocks of tamarind paste at Asian or Indian supermarkets or in the international food section of traditional grocery stores. If you're still unable to find it, you can order from online stores.*

"If you're craving soda, this tamarind sour punch is a nice, natural way to have one without all the sugar and chemicals. It's super refreshing. On a Friday night, I might add a splash of rum and call it a party."

————————————— Angie

CHILLED GUAVA & POMEGRANATE TEA

— Angelo

Though there is technically no tea in this recipe, I call it one because we're infusing light and refreshing flavors into plain water. On really hot summer days, I like to make large batches and sip from tall frosty glasses to keep me hydrated. Serve it at your next backyard barbecue!

SERVES: 4 TO 6
TIM: 25 MINUTES

1 cup guava paste
  (see Tip, page 64)
½ cup honey
2 slices lemon
8 sprigs fresh mint
4 sprigs fresh basil
ice cubes
1 pomegranate, cut in half and
  seeds removed (see Tip)

In a medium saucepan over medium heat, combine the guava paste, honey, and 4 cups water. Bring to a simmer and use a wooden spoon to break up and dissolve the paste. Remove from the heat.

Stir in the lemon slices and half of the mint and basil. Cover and chill in the refrigerator for 15 minutes. Once chilled, strain and pour the tea into glasses filled with ice. Garnish with the remaining mint and basil sprigs and the pomegranate seeds.

Tip HOW TO SEED A POMEGRANATE *My preferred way to remove the seeds, or arils, of a pomegranate is simple: Cut the pomegranate in half. Holding it cut-side down, hit it with the side of a knife. The seeds will easily pop from the fruit. Just make sure to wear an apron; the juice gets everywhere.*

GUAVA BLOODY MARIA
WITH AVOCADO

— Angelo

SERVES: 4
TIME: 5 MINUTES

3 cups tomato juice
3 tablespoons Worcestershire
3 tablespoons fresh lime juice
3 tablespoons Sriracha sauce
¼ cup guava paste (see Tip,
  page 64)
⅓ cup vodka, optional
1 teaspoon kosher salt
ice cubes
1 ripe avocado, peeled,
  seeded, and cubed

You can't go wrong with a classic Bloody Mary, but I wanted to give it a little Latin spin by adding guava paste. The paste adds a sweet dimension to the otherwise savory drink, making it hard to resist. And for a nutritious punch, garnish with chunks of creamy avocado. I like this without alcohol, but feel free to add vodka if you like.

In a pitcher, combine the tomato juice, Worcestershire, lime juice, Sriracha, guava paste, vodka, if using, and salt and mix well.

Place ice cubes in glasses and pour the tomato juice mixture over the ice. Garnish with the avocado cubes.

SOUR GRAPEFRUIT MARGARITA

Angie

The first time I went to Angelo's restaurant Añejo, it was one of those mid-week days when you can't believe you have two more days to go until the weekend. I was meeting my business partner there and was really tempted to back out, but I forced myself to go. When I got there, I ordered a Margarita and with the first sip, I was glad I came! This isn't the same cocktail because Angelo won't give up the secret recipe, but it's pretty close.

SERVES: 2
TIME: 5 MINUTES

coarse salt
1 lime, cut into wedges
1 cup grapefruit juice
½ cup fresh lime juice
¼ cup agave nectar
¼ cup 100% agave tequila,
   such as Clase Azul
   Resposado (see right)
ice cubes

Scatter the salt in a wide, shallow dish. Run a wedge of lime around the rim of two glasses, then dip them in the salt mixture. Set aside.

In a shaker, combine the grapefruit juice, lime juice, agave, and tequila. Drop a handful of ice cubes into the cup and shake well. Carefully strain and pour into the prepared glasses.

HOW TEQUILA IS MADE

Tequila comes from the blue agave, a spiky plant that grows in Mexico. First the agave hearts are roasted in stone ovens. Then they go through maceration, fermentation, and distillation. There are two main categories: 100% Blue Agave or Tequila Mixto (at least 51% blue agave). These are further broken down according to age. The price can vary, but it's always best to look for 100% agave on the label.

NO-GUILT MOJITOS

Angie

I fell in love with Mojitos while visiting Cuba with my mother but then I stopped drinking them because of all the sugar and calories. Eventually I missed the refreshing taste so I worked out this recipe, which is made with agave nectar, a natural sweetener that has less effect on your blood sugar than white sugar, but is 1½ times sweeter so you use less.

SERVES: 1
TIME: 5 MINUTES

½ lime, cut into 4 wedges, plus
   1 wedge for garnish
1½ tablespoons fresh lime juice
2 tablespoons torn fresh mint
   leaves, plus 1 sprig
½ teaspoon agave nectar
2 ounces white rum
4 ounces club soda
ice cubes

Place the lime wedges, lime juice, and mint in a sturdy glass or martini shaker. Crush with a muddler until the mint is well-bruised and fragrant.

Add the agave, rum, and club soda and stir gently. Fill a serving glass with ice cubes and pour the mojito mixture over the ice. Garnish with the extra lime wedge and mint sprig, if desired.

THE IMPORTANCE OF LIME

The lime is the most acidic member of the citrus family; 8% of their weight comes from citric acid, making them extremely sour. Yet limes can brighten up sweet or savory dishes with their refreshing tart flavor and they are rich in vitamin C.

SUMMER SANGRIA
WITH ANCHO & ORANGE

Angelo

If I was ever stranded on a tropical island, I could see myself walking along the beach with a machete in search of a coconut. Once I found a tree, I would climb it, use the machete to cut down a coconut, and hack off the top to reveal the fresh and delicious water so I could make this sangria. Sometimes my imagination can run wild, but I was truly inspired by the beach and heat for this drink. If my daydream is not enticing enough, coconut water is also known for replenishing electrolytes like potassium in the body, and red wine has long been said to benefit the heart.

SERVES: 4
TIME: 5 MINUTES

3 cups dry red wine
½ cup agave nectar
1 cup coconut water
½ cup fresh orange juice
½ cup fresh lime juice
2 dried ancho chile peppers
  (see below)
2 sprigs fresh mint
ice cubes

Combine all the ingredients in a pitcher and stir with a wooden spoon, making sure to break up the mint to release its oils. Chill for 30 minutes and serve over ice.

ANCHO CHILES

Ancho chiles are actually dried poblano peppers. They can be found in the international section of most supermarkets, or order them online.

MANGO & CHIPOTLE SANGRIA

Angelo

Fun and festive, sangrias remind me of hot summer days and backyard barbecues. In this version, I keep it light by using white wine and brightly hued mangoes and oranges. Toss in red grapes to add a burst of sweetness and color. Be sure to let the mixture sit for at least an hour to give the chipotle time to infuse into the wine.

SERVES: 4 TO 6
TIME: 15 MINUTES

2 cups mango chunks (see Tip, page 150)
2 navel oranges, sliced
1 cup seedless red grapes, halved
3 dried chipotle peppers, broken up
1 bottle (750 ml) dry white wine, chilled
½ cup agave nectar
6 sprigs fresh cilantro
ice cubes, optional

Combine all the ingredients in a large pitcher. Using a wooden spoon, mix well. Let sit for at least 1 hour to infuse the liquid with the chipotle peppers. Serve chilled over ice, if desired.

"This is such a fresh, interesting take on sangria. The chipotle adds an unexpected and smoky flavor that's so unusual. I like the fruits Angelo has chosen, but feel free to experiment with other fruits too."

Angie

BARLEY & COCONUT WATER MILKSHAKE

Angelo

Managing two restaurants means I'm often on the phone or running from meeting to meeting. And with my jam-packed days, I sometimes forget to eat. So I devised this drink to enjoy on the run. It's refreshing, extremely filling, and helps boost my energy. Plus, it's made from barley, a whole grain that lends a nutty taste and provides fiber, protein, and iron.

SERVES: 6 TO 8
TIME: 1 HOUR 30 MINUTES

1 cup dried hulled barley
3 cups low-fat (1%) milk
1 cinnamon stick
4 allspice berries
3 cups coconut water
¼ cup agave nectar
ice cubes

In a large sauté pan over medium heat, lightly toast the barley for 5 minutes, continually shaking the pan.

Transfer the barley to a medium saucepan along with the milk, cinnamon stick, and allspice. Cook over low heat until the barley is tender, about 40 minutes. Remove the cinnamon stick and allspice berries and discard.

Transfer the barley mixture to a blender and blend until smooth. Add the coconut water and agave and blend again. Chill in the blender pitcher for 20 to 30 minutes.

Add ice cubes to the chilled mixture and blend until smooth.

NIKO'S
TROPICAL SMOOTHIE

Angie

My son Niko is super sweet, as I know I've already said but it's true! He'll do things for me when I least expect it. Like on Mother's Day, he brought me breakfast in bed, including this smoothie served in a really nice glass. I like that the Greek yogurt has protein and satisfies my hunger in the morning. Plus, it's got naturally sweet and delicious fruit that's worth jumping out of bed for.

SERVES: 1 TO 2
TIME: 5 MINUTES

1 peeled and diced frozen
  mango
1 cup chopped pineapple
1 cup nonfat Greek yogurt
½ cup low-fat (1%) milk
3 to 4 ice cubes

Place all the ingredients in a blender and blend until smooth. Pour into one or two pretty glasses and serve.

INDEX

ACKNOWLEDGMENTS

First and foremost, I'd like to thank Anja Schmidt, Angela Miller, and Kyle Cathie for believing in me, and giving me the opportunity to share my stories and recipes.

I'm so grateful and thankful for the support of my mother and father. I'd also like to thank all of my siblings: Lisa, Pablo, Veronica, Annie, Dolores, and Vicky—I love you all.

To Grandma and Grandpa: I know you're watching over me. Thank you for believing in me and loving me endlessly.

A big thank you to my son Jacob Elias for motivating me to work hard. You are my inspiration.

Thanks to Shirley Fan for dedicating your time to this book and being patient with my schedule.

To Angie: You're amazing. I'm so happy we share the same vision for this book, and I know it will touch the lives of many.

To Robyn Williams, founder of Choice Center, thank you for inspiring to see my vision for my life.

And lastly, to my tía Carmen: You live within me every day I cook. You've inspired me to cook with heart and passion. I love you and miss you.

———————————— *Angelo*

Thank you to my eternally supportive family, I love you more than words: Oronde, Niko, Christian, Mom, Grandma, Tommy, Mel, Cindy, Uncle Steve, Nikki, Rob, John, Jen, Morgan, Steph, Gab, The MG's, CRD, the Waltons, the Costners, the Francos, the Ridingers, the Rocas & the Garrett/Grant family.

Margarita Sullivan, this book is yours, too! You never lost hope and you literally made our vision for HealthyLatinEating.com come alive. Thank you for all that you do!

Kyle Cathie, Anja Schmidt, Shirley Fan, Angela Miller, Diane Perez, and Cameron Kadison—thank you for believing in this project and for all your hard work.

Thank you for sharing!!! DJ Enuff, Rosie Perez, Fat Joe & Lorena Cartagena, John Leguizamo, Chef Alissa Hernandez, Aunt Zunia, Laura & Jorge Posada, Omer Pardillo & the estate of Celia Cruz, Henry Santos, Robinson Cano and Adrienne Bailon—your family recipes are filled with so much love. I'm honored to share them with the world.

Angelo—you are brilliant! And I'm so proud of our book. Thank you forever.

———————————— *Angie*